# PRAISE FOR *LEARNING WITHOU[*

In *Learning without Fear*, Julia and Ruchi tackle some of the myths relating to growth mindset and show how there is much more to this complex field than positive thinking and increased effort alone.

Beautifully illustrated, this terrific book covers the field of growth mindset in a way that is both accessible and thought-provoking – providing subtle insights into the difference between failing and failure, and how to support children to feel comfortable with being uncomfortable, for example. Furthermore, it shares wonderful resources, stories and case studies to help teachers make authentic growth mindset possible for every child in their classroom.

*Learning without Fear* will be incredibly useful for primary school teachers. An absolute gem.

Mary Myatt, education adviser and author of *The Curriculum: Gallimaufry to Coherence*

Forget growth mindset mantras and posters – instead read this more nuanced, comprehensive exploration of a range of strategies designed to achieve success in early years and primary settings.

*Learning without Fear* accessibly and practically describes the critical elements of learning without fear, and also delves into pupil self-regulation and the pitfalls of praising the child rather than the process. It is filled with anecdotes and 'mini stories' – case studies of children's typical negative school experiences or thoughts, skilfully turned into success stories – that all come to life in the book's colourful, welcoming pages, which also feature plenty of research evidence and the authors' personal classroom experiences.

This delightful publication then culminates in a bank of powerful and easy-to-follow lesson ideas, which – together with the rest of the book's content – will help educators develop in their learners a growth mindset that will benefit them both in school and beyond.

Shirley Clarke, international formative assessment expert

*Learning without Fear* is a fantastic introduction to growth mindset in the classroom which skilfully debunks some of its common myths. Accessibly written and based on sound research, the book begins with a discussion on how to assess your own mindset and invites you to consider its impact on your practice. Julia and Ruchi then move on to offer practical ways to introduce the concept of growth mindset to children across the primary school age range, explore its importance as an ethos rather than as a bolt-on lesson, and provide strategies to embed growth mindset throughout the curriculum.

This book will be a valuable addition to the library of both experienced teachers and those new to the profession.

Angela Goodman, Head of School, Waterloo Primary School and part of the #PrimaryRocks team

By distilling a wealth of research on growth mindset and metacognition, *Learning without Fear* provides the classroom teacher with a go-to compendium of ideas and strategies to fully embed a culture of growth in the classroom.

This book has the potential to change every primary school classroom in the land, and should be a key text for any primary teacher training course.

Colin Grimes, teacher, Rothbury First School

A must-read for anybody working with children, *Learning without Fear* offers a fresh approach to looking at growth mindset and provides a whole host of excellent ideas, resources and practical examples. Can teachers make a change? With this book, yes they can!

Graham André, teacher, Lanesend Primary School, speaker,
#PrimaryRocks organiser and eduTwitter influencer

No teacher need be concerned or fearful about developing a growth-mindset philosophy in early years and the primary classroom. *Learning without Fear* has it all here for them.

Nina Jackson, author, award-winning speaker and education consultant, Teach Learn Create Ltd

Julia and Ruchi have produced an instantly accessible, practical guide which explains some of the key concepts central to growth mindset and metacognition in such a way that will help everyone who works with children. The book's mini stories are an excellent medium to get learners to think about different scenarios, and the references to research are useful for anyone who wants to explore the literature around growth mindset in greater depth.

*Learning without Fear* is a really valuable resource which will spark debate and discussion among staff teams and help teachers to reflect on the language they use and the behaviours they model in school.

Ruth Swailes, school improvement adviser and education consultant

If you're interested in optimising the conditions for learning in your classroom, this practical and well-informed guide is a great place to start.

Jonathan Lear, Deputy Head Teacher, St Catherine's Catholic Primary School,
speaker and author of *The Monkey-Proof Box*

# LEARNING WITHOUT FEAR

A Practical Toolkit for Developing Growth Mindset in the Early Years and Primary Classroom

STUCK ISLAND

GROWTH MINDSET

GOT-IT CITY

Julia Stead and Ruchi Sabharwal

First published by

Crown House Publishing
Crown Buildings, Bancyfelin, Carmarthen, Wales, SA33 5ND, UK
**www.crownhouse.co.uk**

and

Crown House Publishing Company LLC
PO Box 2223, Williston, VT 05495, USA
**www.crownhousepublishing.com**

British Library Cataloguing-in-Publication Data

A catalogue entry for this book is available from the British Library.

Print ISBN: 978-178583305-2
Mobi ISBN: 978-178583436-3
ePub ISBN: 978-178583437-0
ePDF ISBN: 978-178583438-7

LCCN 2019940019

Printed and bound in the UK by
Charlesworth Press, Wakefield, West Yorkshire

For John, my dad. A template for life,
and the person who taught me to be fearless. – J. S.

To Ekta and Vibha; my sisters and best friends, who both, in their own unique way, have inspired me to believe that I have a voice worth listening to and who continue to provide the acceptance and safety needed to express that voice. – R. S.

# ACKNOWLEDGEMENTS

As much as I am an adult working alone during lesson time in my island of a class-room, I am never truly in isolation. My acknowledgements run as a two-pronged river. On the first, my teacher self has had plenty of people inspire me to be fearless in my practice, and in my career ambitions. Dave Houghton – my first ever head teacher – who believed that new ways of doing things could work very well, who wrote notes of encouragement regularly during my NQT year, and who left me to it to learn from my own mistakes, thank you. For inspiring colleagues like Janet Worsley, Ros Carter and Estelle Castro, thanks for teaching me things that I wouldn't have learnt on my own. I must also mention the trainee teachers who I have mentored on their first steps of the teaching journey: you taught me how to encourage, mentor and enable. I loved sharing with you. And who would I be without the hundreds of children and families that I have shared my time with over the last 15 years? They are the experts and they are the ones from whom I have everything yet to learn.

The other prong of the river are the people who have enabled this book to be written. To all at Crown House Publishing, thank you for believing in the project, and for being patient while we wrote alongside our teaching commitments. Your wonderful team have been supportive and ever-knowledgeable. To the people who have allowed me space for this book to be researched and written – especially Johanna Partridge, my mum – thank you. To my husband, Darren, thank you for your pride and encourage-ment in all I do. And to the two little case studies who I endeavour to bring up with a mindset disposed towards happiness and self-belief: Alistair and James, you're who this is all about. – J. S.

Teaching is an endless roller coaster of highs and lows, achievements and failures, fear-inducing moments of uncertainty and euphoric flashes of success, but I wouldn't change any of it, for within teaching I have found my fire and my passion, and the classroom has given me a space in which to thrive. It has been a privilege to share my experiences with other teachers and I am humbled that I have been able to express all that I believe about teaching in something as precious as a book. As a young girl I always aspired to write and illustrate my own text, so thank you to all at Crown House Publishing for putting your trust in us and for your unwavering patience. Thank you also to my writing partner, Julia, for pushing us to write a proposal, which we powered through in one sitting. I certainly wouldn't have been brave enough to even imagine that my ramblings would translate into print.

To all the authors of all the books that have guided and encouraged me both profession-ally and personally, without your words to provide friendship, comfort and guidance, I probably wouldn't have pushed myself to strive for the future I have created. To my first ever boss, Darren Smith, for igniting a spark that I hadn't yet felt and suggesting a career in teaching. Thank you for seeing something in me that I couldn't. To my tribe of dedicated colleagues at Dunmow St Mary's Primary School, thank you for pushing me out of my comfort zone, encouraging me to take risks in my classroom and helping me to hone the craft of teaching. Thank you to Becca and Marie for all our debriefs in the prep room, for the shared wisdom, courage, empathy and laughs; you both kept me sane during the tough times, without you both I wouldn't have taken that leap of faith into school leadership. Thank you to Julie Lilly and the entire #LearningFirst community for providing a cause and an audience for my ideas, giving me the positive feedback that I needed in order to dare greatly. Without you I never would have had the audacity to put my ideas to paper. To my oldest friend, Michelle, for all the long-distance support and lengthy conversations about writing which helped me to overcome that initial blank page. To Sarah May, for forever championing me and helping me to see that my accomplishments are valid and deserved. To all the pupils and parents I have engaged with over the years, who have each had a hand in shaping who I am as a teacher – in particular to the last class I taught full-time. I watched you develop into impassioned, inquisitive and collaborative learners, and saw you reaching beyond any limitations set by those who couldn't truly see what you were made of. If this book aspires to do anything, it's to help ensure that more pupils are nurtured to harness their potential so they can achieve well beyond their expectations. To all the other supporting characters I have met and the relationships we have developed along the way (you know who you are), thank you for each teaching me something about myself which has undoubtedly contributed to my compassion as a teacher.

Finally, thank you to my family, particularly my parents. To Mom for your unconditional faith and guidance and to Papa for teaching me the value of hard work. To my husband Adam for being a continuous source of encouragement and support. Your IT skills, eye for proofreading, countless cups of tea and endless patience have made all of this pos-sible. Thank you for helping me to see that I could get there in the end. Finally, to my two little miracles. I hope you grow up to be as fearless and resilient as I know you can be. I can't wait to meet you. – R. S.

# CONTENTS

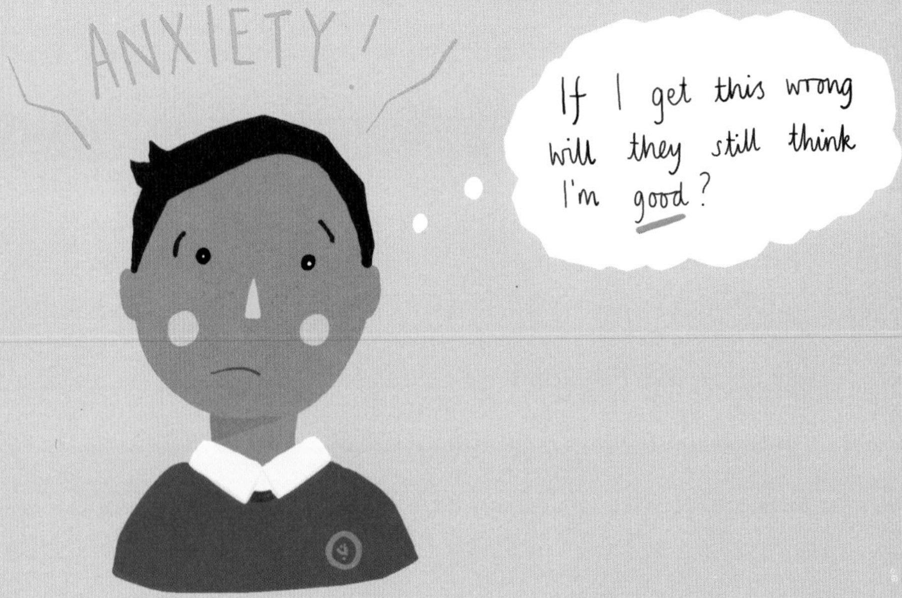
ANXIETY!
If I get this wrong will they still think I'm good?

# INTRODUCTION

This is a book that has grown out of our experiences in the classroom, our further reading and our professional dialogue, so it seems logical to start by introducing ourselves. We're Julia Stead and Ruchi Sabharwal, and between us we have over 20 years' experience in the primary classroom, right through from Reception to Year 6. We share a passion for teaching and learning and, when we began discussing our pedagogy and practice – and realised the effect we were having on our learners – concluded that it was worth sharing our ideas. So we started writing this book. Here we each draw on examples from our own classrooms and experience, which are woven alongside insights from our wider reading and brought to life with Ruchi's colourful illustrations, which are available to download to use in the classroom.

One day, we were sat discussing the atmosphere in our classrooms. Ruchi reflected, 'So often in my classroom learning feels stunted because the children sat in front of me are scared. Scared to ask, to try, to question and to challenge. Scared of getting it wrong, of being slow, of looking stupid, of letting their teacher down and of being exposed as anything other than clever, right or "good".'

We agreed that every single pupil we've ever taught has experienced moments in which they were inhibited by fear, and some never quite got over it. But surely this wasn't good enough! We knew that these children hadn't always felt like this. As babies and toddlers, they were inquisitive explorers of the world around them, bold in their risk-taking and courageous when it came to pushing through failures and trying again. So what happened? At what point did the intrinsic curiosity of very young children become stifled? Was it in the classroom? Through exposure to competition? When did our pupils become self-conscious about their *ability*?

It was rather serendipitous that Ruchi stumbled across growth mindset in the work of Carol Dweck when she was sent on a course about teaching success.[1] She is so grateful to the perceptive head teacher who sent her on it, because that day changed her life, and she thinks the head knew that it would. It might sound dramatic but believe her when she says that sitting with a group of like-minded colleagues who challenged and

---

1   Carol S. Dweck, *Mindset: The New Psychology of Success* (London: Random House, 2006).

debated their own approaches to teaching and learning, and understood the impact this could have, gave her career a huge injection of agency.

Anyway, after discovering growth mindset, Ruchi started to think about her own fixed mindset and how this had inhibited her growth. Throughout her experiences in school, for whatever reason, she had convinced herself that she was not a mathematician and that she couldn't do certain things. So, of course, she never even tried. She would rather avoid something altogether instead of risking messing it up and, worse still, risking others finding out that she wasn't as good as they thought. What she realised through reading Dweck's work was that she was limiting her options because of her fear. This was a real light-bulb moment and she quickly realised how powerful it could've been if her own growth mindset had been nurtured at an early age. If she wanted to be a mathematician, there was no reason for her not to try and work at it. As it turns out, she absolutely loves teaching maths now and it's because she has worked hard, tried new approaches, developed new ways of teaching and learnt with her pupils. Before this, if you caught her on a maths course or in a meeting, she would've sat at the back – cocooned in her own fear of failing and avoiding questions at all costs. In fact, she probably wouldn't have even attempted to interact for fear of her colleagues seeing her flop and then immediately asking her to kindly leave the profession and close the door on her way out. If teachers feel that way, imagine how the pupils feel when they are quizzed on their seven times table and are expected to give an answer within three seconds! She revealed this fear to Julia, who, of course, had experienced the same feeling.

For adults, this feeling is often referred to as 'imposter syndrome', the psychological belief that despite proven competence and success, you are inadequate and that any achievements you have had have been down to sheer luck.[2] This leads to the fear that one day your luck will run out and you will be uncovered as a fraud. In schools, the threat of exposure is hard to avoid because teachers have nowhere to hide; our successes and failures are transparent to all and we are highly accountable. It is so important for teachers to embrace the mindset principles we are trying to encourage our pupils to adopt.

So, one course and countless books later, not only did the weight of our professional influence and moral responsibility truly hit us, but the fundamental belief that the link between mindset and success fed into all aspects of learning landed full-force too. We

---

2    Angela Watson, 7 Ways Teachers Can Push Past Imposter Syndrome, *The Cornerstone for Teachers* [blog] (12 November 2017). Available at: https://thecornerstoneforteachers.com/truth-for-teachers-podcast/imposter-syndrome/.

knew we had to develop ways of weaving this into every strand of classroom life, and we wanted to make sure that there was impact in our endeavour. This meant rethinking how we taught, understanding when to sit back and thinking carefully about our questions. Underpinning this was the sky-high expectations we held of *all* our pupils. So much so that they started to hold them of themselves. What we learnt during the two years that we dedicated to refining this approach with two classes of Year 3 pupils was that although children can be extremely resilient, this is too easily challenged; it takes very little to switch a child off from learning. We understood how quickly a learner can label themselves, feeling incapable or that they are not worthy or good enough. This can happen in a split second, in the middle of an English lesson on a Wednesday morning, when everything had been going fine and you least expected it. But the moment a child feels stupid is the moment they can become disaffected. It can be a fight to bring them back if you don't notice and act quickly.

On the other hand, we also learnt – and wanted to share with others, hence the motivation for writing this book – that through flipping your thinking, by bringing everything you do back to learning, by modelling success and failure, and by letting go and giving your pupils opportunities to explore, you can achieve some truly amazing things together. Through careful planning, differentiation and assessment you have the absolute power to transform learning behaviours. It is not always easy and we face challenges that can get in the way sometimes, but it is very possible and the strategies for doing so are in this book.

The words, 'Have a growth mindset!' were rarely used in our classrooms. Instead, what we developed was a little learning community, in which children genuinely felt pride when they tried, regardless of the outcome. This was the first stepping stone to making our pupils braver. When they felt brave, they wanted to be challenged, they wanted to be independent and they wanted to know how to get better. The biggest achievement with our classes was in nurturing positive relationships, and in how well all the children worked with each other. There was no fear of competition: over time, through our classroom communities, we learnt each other's strengths and used collaboration as a conduit to improvement. The more we worked together and allowed space for everyone's ideas, the more confidence emanated from even those pupils who had never experienced this feeling before. Over time, through the methods outlined in this book, pupils who previously felt too anxious to share their answers felt safe enough to participate, and everyone wanted to listen. We are so proud of these pupils and, although we've been teaching for many years between us, we feel that we learnt an awful lot from them too.

Although growth mindset has been talked about in education for long enough now that most teachers and schools see the benefit in adopting the principles, what we really want you to take away from this book is that relationships really do lie at the heart of everything we do in the classroom. Forget posters about how great mistakes are, and superficial encouragement about perseverance. Changing a *mindset* goes so much deeper than taking some ideas from Twitter or Pinterest. Here you will find a practical model that you can use to start embedding some of the qualities associated with a growth mindset. But hopefully this is just the starting point for you and, together with your class, you will discover your own nuggets of greatness and success that will form the basis of your very own learning community. We urge you to continue the legacy and share any successes, no matter how small, with your colleagues because you might just light the spark of an ember that was already glowing and – without even realising it – inspire someone else to take a risk.

## Chapter 1

# BRAIN VS MINDSET

Imagine for a moment that you are learning to drive for the first time (if you've never been behind the wheel, stay with us, there's plenty for you later). Although you are determined, you are having problems with the accelerator and the clutch. You know that you can't engage them both at the same time – your instructor keeps barking this at you every time you stall – and yet your feet are not receiving this message. Your nerves are increasing, you feel hot and sweaty, and you're gripping that steering wheel like your life depends on it. *Left foot down, first gear, right foot on the accelerator, slowly raise my left foot off the clutch, handbrake off and we're moving. Now into second gear, left foot down* ... and you've done it again. The engine is off, your instructor has that now-familiar look of exasperation and you've sworn off driving for life.

So what now? What is the single most important thing you can do to try to overcome this obstacle?

Persevere!

Believe in yourself!

Bounce back!

Try again!

Practise!

Work harder!

(Altogether now:) Have a *growth mindset*!

Well, yes to all the above, but the answer is much simpler and more practical. First, in order to rectify your mistake, you need to recognise *where* you are going wrong and *why*. The only way to do that is to widen your knowledge and understanding of the car. The key to improvement is to take an active role in your own learning, starting with the clutch and understanding how it works. Okay, so accessing and processing this information isn't going to miraculously make you a perfect driver, but it *will* get you thinking, noticing and, in time, self-correcting. Even if you think you are not mechanically minded, it doesn't matter; you don't need to be an expert. During the first stages of the learning process, holding a rudimentary understanding of the mechanism is enough of an insight to get you through the difficulty.

In the early days of learning to drive, long-term 'mastery' knowledge of engineering is not necessary. Noticing a few distinct engine sounds, knowing when the gear needs changing and identifying the point at which to put your left foot down all goes towards increasing your confidence, and is enough to get you through the basics. In time, your confidence with and control of your vehicle will grow. You will probably gain a better understanding of your car and how to get the best out of its functionality – for example, why the quality of fuel affects the performance, why a consistently lower speed is more efficient, and so on. The more we know about what is going on with the machine, the more we know what to do in order to optimise our driving and the performance of the car. Formula One drivers, for instance, have a far greater understanding of how to optimise their vehicle than the average driver does.

Greater understanding of the car = using the car more effectively = better driver

That's all well and good but we promised you a chapter on the brain and mindset – not on racing – so what on earth does driving have to do with that? Well, the chances are that you are reading this book because you are passionate about teaching and learning, you want to teach your pupils in a way that makes them successful lifelong learners, and you are curious about how to utilise the concept of growth mindset in order to do that, right? Driving a car is an analogy for the only logical place from which we can start to unpick mindset: the brain. The basic principles of neuroplasticity – meaning that the brain can adapt, change and form new connections in response to its environment – are the foundations of mindset theory and, hence, it's crucial to start our journey here.

Non-drivers still with us? Let's take the body and its organs and systems. While deepening our understanding of the digestive system won't have any direct impact on how hungry or satiated we are, engaging our brains to understand what types of food will keep us fuller for longer allows us to make informed choices about what we put into our bodies to ensure we feel full and satisfied.

Greater understanding of bodily functions = improved choices about how we use our body = healthier and more effective human

In the same way, if we can engage our brains to *learn about* our brains – this is metacognition, which we'll discuss in more detail later – we can start to: actively exercise, change and shape how our brains work; take control of our 'abilities'; and revolutionise the effectiveness of our learning. It's pretty powerful stuff, almost magical, especially when we realise that we each have the potential to physically expand our neural pathways and change the way in which our brains perform.

Greater understanding of the brain = using brain processes more effectively = better learner

# GREY MATTERS

First off, let us reassure you that, as complicated as it may sound, you don't need to be a neuroscientist to understand or teach this next bit. If you have studied science or psychology, you can feel very smug at this point as you probably already know what we're about to say, and we apologise in advance if this explanation is slightly rudimentary. When we first started reading about mindset, we found many in-depth, scholarly articles on learning theories and although the research into neuroplasticity was fascinating, we needed to break it down further for our own comprehension. So we shall attempt to do that here.

The human brain is an extremely complex and amazingly powerful organ, which functions as an intricate network, with each synaptic link charged and able to reorganise itself by forming new connections between existing brain cells. It has the capacity to shift and develop by absorbing information quickly. We've often heard the brain referred to as 'elastic', 'stretchy' and 'malleable' and this is the essence of neuroplasticity. It describes the long-lasting functional shifts in the brain and its, rather outstanding, ability to change or 'rewire' its neural pathways.

*Hang on, what's a neural pathway?*

Okay, good question. Put your thinking caps on, we're going to go a bit deeper.

Neurons are nerve cells in the brain that carry information in the form of tiny electrical signals. Neurons carry signals and impulses and this allows us to process sensory information. Neurons communicate with each other by sending chemicals called neurotransmitters across small gaps called synapses in order to form connections. If we use the same synaptic connections often enough, we form a brand-new neural pathway. It's very sophisticated stuff, a bit like the World Wide Web only even more important.

Neuroplasticity works through neurons firing and fusing, and this happens throughout our lives through our experiences, through learning new things and through memorising new information. The brain is exceptionally good at adapting. When it experiences something new it responds to sensory stimulation by reorganising the neural circuitry, and a change occurs in its structure. In other words, through specific use, we can actively *grow* our brains (cue gasps from the audience). Pretty amazing stuff.

As we get older that huge brain-growing potential depletes, and only the stronger connections that we use more frequently remain. Think of it as 'synaptic pruning' in which only the strongest links will survive.[1] The brain is very resourceful and will filter out what it thinks is irrelevant, especially information that we don't regularly use. Obviously, this explains why Ruchi can't really remember much of her undergraduate dissertation. Use it or lose it, as the saying goes.

Neuroplasticity occurs during specific phases:

1. During the early stages of development as the immature brain organises itself. This explains why babies, toddlers and young children are able to learn and retain so much, so quickly. Earlier in our development, it is easier for the brain to form new connections. These are also the ones that tend to stick the longest.

2. In adulthood whenever something new is learnt, repeated and memorised.

3. In the case of brain injury to compensate for lost functions. If necessary, the brain is able to dedicate its resources to specific functions and, at times, rewire itself to compensate for the damage done.

---

1 Edalmarys Santos and Chad A. Noggle, Synaptic Pruning. In Sam Goldstein and Jack A. Naglieri (eds), *Encyclopedia of Child Behavior and Development* (Boston, MA: Springer, 2011), pp. 1464–1465.

4.  In response to genetic factors, the characteristics of our environment and, most significantly, our own actions.

As an interesting anecdote, upon asking Ruchi's non-teaching sister to proofread the above, she patiently complied and after a couple of minutes said, 'I think I get it, but I'm going to have to read it a couple of times. It's just the way my brain works; I don't understand things like that straight away.' Ruchi smiled knowingly and told her that she was, in some ways, the target reader for this book. Her understanding was nothing to do with her brain, but rather what she thinks and believes about her brain. Through her idea to reread the section a few times, she showed excellent growth mindset potential – practice is a key trait, as you will find out later. But to help you (and Ruchi's sister) out, let's think of it another way.

Imagine a country park, with ponds, pathways through the woods, a few fields, a picnic spot, etc. Got it? Okay, now visualise it as a dynamic, living organism, shifting and changing as more and more people use it. Children start exploring different ways through the wood – they carry sticks to make dens and this forms new offshoot paths. A new path appears from the pond to the picnic area. Because these appealing little paths become well-trodden by inquisitive wellied feet, people start using them instead of the original ones. Eventually, the original paths get overgrown and nobody remembers they were there.

With us so far? Hold onto your hats.

Neuroplasticity offers us an explanation of what happens in our brains whenever we are doing anything new. Everything we do is shaping and changing the brain as it responds to the information the five senses give it. Imagine how much change we could bring about by being *aware*, by giving it the rich and diverse information it craves in order to evolve in such a dynamic way. We could say that neuroplasticity explicitly refers to one aspect of the science of how our brains work – and their ability to transform – while mindset refers to our psychology, or our beliefs about how our brains work.

This makes more sense when we look at how neural pathways were previously understood. Until we started unpicking mindset and the effect on learners, it felt natural to assume that as we aged, the connections formed in our brains remained fixed. Have you ever tried to do something that you haven't done for a long time and someone helpfully comes out with, 'It's like riding a bike, you never forget!' Well, actually, you can and, as it turns out, it's completely normal to forget how to split the bill for dinner five ways if you haven't done mental maths since your GCSEs ten years ago. Blame synaptic pruning.

Plasticity is the brain's wonderful gift of changing through learning and it completely debunks the idea that ability or learning is fixed and unchangeable. In fact, those pathways adapt specifically to what we think and do. The neurons ignite and the synapses fuse whenever we learn, practise or master new skills. And guess what? You can help this to happen by allowing your mindset to change and believing that you can change your learning outcomes. The more you practise something tricky, the more likely it is that a new neural pathway will form. Persevere and it will become even stronger. Your tenacity and resilience aid the formation of a well-trodden path in the country park.

This theory is backed up by a notable comparative study which looked at the brains of London taxi drivers and London bus drivers. Through brain scans, scientists observed evidence of neuroplasticity and found that taxi drivers typically had a larger hippocampus – the part of the brain involved with storing long-term memory, knowledge and experiences – than the bus drivers did. This was because the taxi drivers had regularly exercised this part of the brain in order to form an extremely comprehensive mental map of London, which they needed in order to perform their job effectively. Bus drivers were used to restricted routes and didn't need to make as many spatial or locational connections as their counterparts in the study.[2] It seems the test that London cabbies have to take is not called 'the Knowledge' for nothing.

This investigation is one part of an extensive body of research which concludes that the brain is like any other muscle in the body: it develops, strengthens and improves the more it is used. This leads to the development of new neurons and the formation of new neural pathways – also known as neurogenesis, to give it its superhero name. Neurogenesis can be simply defined as the growth and development of nervous tissue. When you become an expert at a specific skill, or develop a particularly deep knowledge base, the areas in your brain that deal with this type of processing will increase in size – like the hippocampi of the London taxi drivers – all because of the formation of the new pathways.

---

2   Eleanor A. Maguire, Katherine Woollett and Hugo J. Spiers, London Taxi Drivers and Bus Drivers: A Structural MRI and Neuropsychological Analysis, *Hippocampus*, 16(12) (2006): 1091–1101.

# MINDSET MATTERS

Okay, we've got the science stuff out of the way; we know *what* we need to get our pupils' (and our own) brains to do. Now we need to know *how* we get them to do it. This leads us nicely into the meaty bit and the part where it all starts to come together: growth and fixed mindsets, and the link with brain power and intelligence.

Before we start, we feel that the following paragraph needs a disclaimer. What we are about to say is not intended to shame or expose any of our colleagues who are trying their absolute best to do their jobs with the highest levels of enthusiasm, passion and integrity, most of whom categorically place their pupils at the core of every new strategy they bring into the classroom. We know that teachers work incredibly hard to do things right by their pupils, and that their hearts are nearly always in the right place despite the increasing burdens that are put upon them. That's one of the many reasons why we love our profession. Seriously, guys – we're all doing a really good job. However, sometimes, time constraints and the external pressure to adopt yet another new 'learning policy' that senior management have plucked out of their bag of tricks, leads us all (your authors included) to bulldoze an approach into our classrooms without careful research, thought or attention. It seems that, despite our good intentions, growth mindset is one such concept.

The term 'growth mindset' has become a bit of a buzz phrase in recent years, something that 'you can dip in and out of with your pupils if you have a spare half hour or a PSHE slot to fill' (as a colleague said to Julia once). We have been into a lot of classrooms and spoken to a lot of teachers who have attended specific continuing professional development (CPD) sessions on growth mindset or been genuinely inspired by something they have read and wanted to try it out. Bravo to that. We wholeheartedly encourage a proactive approach to research-led, evidence-based teaching and to the sharing of strategies, ideas and dialogue within our professional community. But we have also seen teachers confuse the research – or pick it up at surface level – at which point, growth mindset becomes synonymous with 'try harder', 'more effort' or 'positive thinking'. This is where we start to worry.

## Carol Dweck

> For twenty years, my research has shown that the view you adopt of yourself profoundly affects the way you lead your life.
>
> Carol Dweck[3]

It's true that how we see ourselves and our own potential shapes how successful we will become. Carol Dweck theorised this in her seminal book *Mindset: The New Psychology of Success*. However, it's sometimes easy to misunderstand this as simply needing to *believe* that you can achieve, never giving up on a task — even when this starts to hinder learning — or telling each other that sticking 'yet' onto the end of 'Miss, I can't do this' is enough. We're sorry to break it to you, but in isolation these strategies simply aren't going to work for you or your pupils. Growth mindset is so much more than 'yet'.

When Dweck wrote about mindset she was talking about the view we adopt of ourselves, from as young as four years old, and about how these beliefs have the power to limit our potential or enable our success. It can mark the difference between outstanding and mediocre, influence our self-awareness and our resilience in the face of obstacles or challenges, determine our levels of grit and determination and, ultimately, impact our self-esteem. She categorised these self-beliefs into two groups.

| Mindset | Fixed | Growth |
|---|---|---|
| **Your belief** | Brain power and intelligence are fixed traits and what we are born with is what we are stuck with. | Brain power and intelligence are cultivated through regular use of a set of learning habits — including practice, effort, challenge and reflection. |
| **Your priority** | Look clever, not stupid. Don't take risks or challenge yourself in case you fail. | Become clever through learning, deliberately taking risks and stepping out of your comfort zone. |

3   Dweck, *Mindset*, p. 6.

| Mindset | Fixed | Growth |
| --- | --- | --- |
| **You feel intelligent when** | You are achieving easy, low-effort successes and outperforming others. You can finish tasks quickly and get everything right. | You are engaging fully with new concepts, exerting effort, stretching and applying your skills. You can develop skills through a variety of tasks. |
| **You avoid** | Effort, mistakes, difficulty or setbacks because if you are clever then things should come easily to you.<br><br>Higher-performing peers who may outshine you and expose your weaknesses or mistakes. | Easy, previously mastered tasks because it leads to boredom and disengagement, and caps your learning power. |

If we think back to how our brains work, if we view ourselves as non-mathematicians and shy away from maths challenges due to fear of failure, over time there is the danger of this becoming a self-fulfilling prophecy as our confidence and resilience in maths reduces. A child who struggles in maths is reinforcing this bias every time they struggle or feel like they can't manage a task. The messages we tell ourselves are clearly not going to help us feel confident about the maths task that crops up in the next lesson. Throughout childhood, Ruchi felt (and told herself) that she 'wasn't a science or maths person'. She convinced herself that this was just the way she was and that it was perfectly normal and acceptable because writing and art was where she flourished – textbook fixed mindset. The problem with that was that she was scared about her peers and teachers 'finding out' her weaknesses. With the benefit of hindsight, she can see this now. The good education she was privileged to receive helped her overcome this idea. As an adult, having learnt about mindset, she now understands the neuroscientific concepts behind growth mindset. It just goes to show that when you are led down a route of thinking that 'ability' can be changed – that you are in charge of learning something in a way that suits you – you can overcome these perceptions and remove the limits you once placed on yourself.

Without blowing her own trumpet, Ruchi was a bit of a high-achiever in most areas at school and managed to feign accomplishment in science until the middle of secondary school when things began to get a bit harder and she was terrified. To feel good about herself, she needed to 'look clever' at all costs. Looking clever meant praise from teachers, peers and parents and this was critical for her feelings of self-worth. So she never put herself forward for challenges for fear of getting it wrong and having all those lovely warm feelings of external praise dissipate. She stuck to what she knew she could do, took things slowly and shied away from asking questions. 'I shouldn't need to ask questions as I should always know what I am doing.' She was completely stationary in this area of her learning. What changed that was encountering the work on mindsets from which this book stems.

In your classroom, fixed and growth mindsets may manifest in the traits outlined in the table that follows. Spend a week listening to and observing the learning habits of your pupils. Become something of a mindset detective and see if you can spot any of these characteristics. It's worth mentioning that it is very possible, and likely, for all of us to sit in the middle of the beliefs, or for an individual's mindset to fluctuate depending on the area they are exploring. So Dylan in Year 3 might have a fixed mindset about gymnastics, for instance. Perhaps he feels nervous or worried that others will see him struggle so he avoids climbing the ropes or sticks to the second bar on the climbing apparatus, when you believe he could go higher. But in design technology (DT) lessons, he's a different child. He will go over to other children to see what they are doing and ask for tips. He might seek out feedback or guidance from you on his cutting techniques as he's finding it difficult to guide the scissors when cutting out different shapes. He feels really proud of himself when he finally manages to cut out a Christmas tree without a single rip. He has higher levels of resilience and personal drive in these lessons than you've ever observed in gymnastics.

| Fixed mindset | Growth mindset |
| --- | --- |
| You feel an urgency to prove yourself. | You feel a desire to learn because you believe that you can improve through practice. |
| You avoid challenges. | You embrace challenges. |

| Fixed mindset | Growth mindset |
|---|---|
| You give up easily in the face of challenge. | You stick at a task, even if it is not going well: setbacks don't discourage you. |
| You see effort as pointless. | You see effort as the path to mastery. |
| You disregard useful or negative feedback. | You actively ask for feedback and use this to move on. |
| You hate criticism: you might even see it as an attack on your character. | You welcome constructive criticism. |
| You hate making mistakes. | You seek to understand and learn from your mistakes. |
| You feel threatened by the success of others, particularly if you have failed in the same task. | You find lessons and inspiration in the success of others. |
| You may reach high levels of academic attainment, but you achieve less than your full potential. | You make sustained progress and can reach higher levels of achievement. |
| You have a deterministic view of the world – it is how it is and cannot be changed. | You believe that hard work, practice and effort are the keys to success. |

Imagine how this plays out in a classroom. Anders was described as a 'bright boy' by his previous teacher. 'He's one of your higher-ability children, especially in maths. He's got a maths brain on him. He was doing calculations with four-digit numbers by the end of Year 2.' You can presume that Anders has been told about his 'maths brain' for most of his young life. When you start to teach him, you notice that he's keen and willing. He whizzes through the tasks you've given him, proudly announcing that it was all 'easy'. When you present him with an appropriate challenge aimed at making him think and developing his skills, something changes. His facial expression shifts and his body language becomes closed. He's stuck and he doesn't like it. He disengages, maybe starts to distract his partner – anything to avoid doing the task at hand. It's obvious that Anders' fixed mindset is impeding his potential. On the surface, this doesn't seem like a big thing to tackle.

On the flip side, Amelia has taken on board all your messages about mistakes being great for learning, and about failure just being part of the learning process. She's on board with challenges and she's got bundles of enthusiasm. The problem is that Amelia hasn't fully understood why mistakes are so great. The challenges she's choosing aren't actually right for this stage of her learning journey. You think she's ticking the growth boxes, but actually her mindset is still fixed because she's choosing those trickier questions for you: to impress, to get a smile or a well done from her teacher.

You begin to realise that perhaps the mindset chat at the beginning of the year just wasn't enough to develop beneficial learning habits. Praising Amelia's effort, rather than her or her outcomes, was a great boost at the beginning, but it has lost meaning and momentum. Her progress is stuck. She's saying the right things, but it isn't enough. In Amelia we can see *extrinsic* motivation at play. She is motivated by your praise, or by stickers, or by the belief that doing what you – the teacher – wants is what will make her successful. Extrinsic motivation means Amelia is motivated by things outside of herself. Things that, actually, she can't control. The opposite – *intrinsic* motivation – is the goal. We want Amelia to want to learn because of the reward she feels inside for finally managing to grasp something. She's not learning for the good of her teacher; she's learning because she wants to know more, she wants to understand more, and because understanding feels good to her – intrinsically.

If children are exposed to saccharine levels of praise for adopting cherry-picked growth-mindset mantras without proper understanding or depth, this can actually exacerbate some of the very problems that growth mindset is intended to counter. This kind of feedback – and what to say instead – is discussed at length in Chapter 8. The problem is not in praising effort itself, but in the omission of explicitly showing how the effort creates learning progress or successful outcomes. Remember that the psychology of learning is affected by lots of internal and external factors; our job is to help our pupils change their internalised ideas about learning and their own potential as much as possible.

What's interesting is that as soon as you become aware of fixed and growth mindsets and familiarise yourself with the traits and nuances of each one, it becomes so much easier to spot the mindsets of the pupils you teach. We have often found that the higher achievers in school, the ones who have been told from a very early age that they are 'clever', 'bright' or 'smart', are more likely to possess fixed mindsets because they've never had to try before: things come easily to them and they get praise for it. Their self-worth is centred on their intelligence and, particularly for those children who rarely experience failure in their formative years, they have very low levels of resilience. Hence they find it much harder to bounce back from difficulties, a bit like Ruchi with science.

Ruchi remembers a boy called Otis, who she taught in Year 4. His parents worked in academia, his big sister was very successful at school and there were a lot of hidden pressures on his little shoulders. He had such a fixed view of his abilities that he just couldn't handle anyone offering help or guidance if he had done something wrong. He'd often sit in the most uncomfortable position in an attempt to cover his work because he couldn't cope with other children looking at and 'copying' his precious ideas. He would argue with his peers if they had done well and he hadn't, and it led to a lot of anxiety about 'looking smart'. He worked hard for others' acceptance and rarely for himself. We guarantee that everyone reading this has taught – or will teach – someone like Otis and, as teachers, it is difficult to know what to do (there is light at the end of this story, don't worry).

It took time but by the end of that year – through all the strategies you will read about – Otis did make progress and he did develop some metacognitive strategies which led to increased levels of independence and confidence. He started to learn that it was good to share your ideas because you can inspire others to build upon them and offer even more in collaboration. Through the celebration of mistakes, he learnt that being comfortable in the realms of what you can already do means you're not learning new skills. That behaviour didn't feel very 'clever' to him once he'd had that realisation. Trust us when we say that this stuff works. The not-so-good news is that before you even attempt it with your pupils, you need to look at your own mindset and your own 'mindset triggers'. Where do you sit? Do you have a fixed mindset about your pupils and their abilities or potential? In one interview Dweck says:

> I think a lot of what happened [with false growth mindset among educators] is that instead of taking this long and difficult journey, where you work on understanding your triggers, working with them, and over time being able to stay in a growth mindset more and more, many educators just said, 'Oh yeah, I have a growth mindset' because either they know it's the right mindset to have or they understood it in a way that made it seem easy. […] Often when we see kids who aren't learning well, we might feel frustrated or defensive, thinking it reflects on us as educators. It's often tempting to not feel it is our fault. So we might say the child has a fixed mindset, without understanding instead that, as educators, it is our responsibility to create a context in which a growth mindset can flourish.[4]

> This article was originally published on the website TheAtlantic.com and is republished here with *The Atlantic*'s permission.

The good news is that you've started in the right place with this book. Together, we can start to tackle that left-hand column on pages 14–15 through the explicit teaching of often-hidden skills. You are going to learn some strategies to change the climate and culture of learning in your classroom, teach your pupils *how* to nourish a growth mindset and show them that, from this, their intelligence, skillset and knowledge will flourish.

---

4   Quoted in Christine Gross-Loh, How Praise Became a Consolation Prize, *The Atlantic* (16 December 2016). Available at: https://www.theatlantic.com/education/archive/2016/12/how-praise-became-a-consolation-prize/510845/.

## Chapter 2
# GETTING STARTED

The journey we'll take in this book is designed to support you in introducing, developing and embedding growth mindset in your classroom or school. It treads a logical, chronological route, so each chapter helps you build on what you've read previously. Knowing where you are right now will help you to begin from an honest starting point. The graphic that follows was introduced to Julia when she mentored trainee teachers. It is a good explanation of how we are unaware of what we don't know when we first start to learn something – what's called unconscious incompetence. As we progress, we start to realise what there is to learn. We know what the content is, but we haven't fully learnt it yet – conscious incompetence. After we've done some work or study, we have an understanding of the subject and are aware of this new knowledge – conscious competence. Finally, we get to the point where we are so au fait with the new knowledge that it becomes second nature to us. It is integrated as part of our behaviour and knowledge bank and will last long into the future – unconscious competence. Right now, you might be unconsciously incompetent – you don't yet know what you don't know. As you move through the book – and get to grips with the ideas, steps and resources – you'll discover more and become more consciously aware of the practices you can adopt in your classroom.

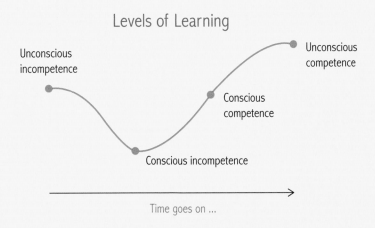

Levels of Learning

Unconscious incompetence

Unconscious competence

Conscious competence

Conscious incompetence

Time goes on ...

In adopting a growth-mindset-influenced teaching and learning environment, there are lots of things to learn to do differently, even if you credit yourself with a growth mindset from the outset. We need to be self-reflective and self-aware from the start, so the questionnaire that follows is the first rung of that self-awareness ladder. We can't help the children to adapt their mindset and learning behaviours until we know who *we* are first.

We have called it a *staff* questionnaire because growth mindset benefits everyone in the school. It isn't just teachers who are responsible for nurturing it: teaching assistants (TAs) and staff who work outside the classroom have a role to play too. Having said that, the questionnaire is aimed at those who participate in, and have an impact on, lessons and learning.

# STAFF QUESTIONNAIRE

Please give yourself a score to indicate the extent to which you agree with each of the following statements. 0 is completely disagree; 10 is absolutely agree.

1. I believe that intelligence can be improved.

2. I encourage my pupils to value the effort that they put into a task higher than the end result.

3. I am comfortable with pupils making mistakes in the classroom.

4. I am happy to let my pupils see me making mistakes.

5. I give feedback to pupils in ways that show them their effort is being rewarded.

6. I understand how to avoid nurturing perfectionism in my pupils.

7. The pupils in my class discuss their learning challenges in a positive way.

8. I am aware of how certain words and labels can be conducive, or become a barrier, to growth mindset in my pupils.

9.   I can recognise which pupils have a fixed mindset by how they respond to challenges and hard work.

10.  I do not accept mediocrity in my pupils' work.

If your score is 100, then you're nearly a finished product in terms of growth mindset. Realistically though, you're likely to have a more modest score which will show you where you are on the continuum of growth mindset knowledge and practice.

⟵————————————————————————————⟶

**Novice: 0**                                                                 **Expert: 100**

Some theoretical knowledge.

Have read some growth-mindset-related stories and discussed them.

Have an active display.

Children can talk about some growth mindset principles.

Can see some change in the mindset of some pupils.

Feel confident about how to help change children's mindsets.

# KEY STAGE 1 PUPIL QUESTIONNAIRE

Please read the questions to the children and ask them to circle 'true' or 'false'.

| | | | |
|---|---|---|---|
| 1. | I like it when my work is a bit tricky sometimes. | True | False |
| 2. | I only feel good if I get all the answers right. | True | False |
| 3. | Mistakes can be good sometimes. | True | False |
| 4. | I want everyone to know when I have got everything right. | True | False |
| 5. | It's fun when we learn something brand new. | True | False |
| 6. | I get worried if I don't understand something. | True | False |
| 7. | I always try my best. | True | False |
| 8. | Some people find everything easy because they are just really clever. | True | False |
| 9. | I can get better at anything by working hard. | True | False |
| 10. | If the learning is tricky, the best thing to do is ask the teacher to tell you how to do it. | True | False |

# KEY STAGE 2 PUPIL QUESTIONNAIRE

Please read the questions and think about whether the sentence describes you or not. Put a ring around 'true' if you agree with the statement, or 'false' if you don't agree.

| | | | |
|---|---|---|---|
| 1. | I like it when my work is a bit tricky sometimes. | True | False |
| 2. | I only feel good about my learning if I get all the answers correct. | True | False |
| 3. | Mistakes can be good sometimes. | True | False |
| 4. | I feel proudest when people think I'm clever for getting the answers right. | True | False |
| 5. | It's fun when we learn something brand new, because we all have to start from nothing. | True | False |
| 6. | I get worried if I don't understand something. | True | False |
| 7. | I always try my best because anything less than my best is a waste of effort. | True | False |
| 8. | Some people find everything easy because they are just really clever. | True | False |
| 9. | I can get better at anything if I work hard enough at it – practice makes perfect! | True | False |
| 10. | If the learning is tricky, the best thing to do is ask the teacher to tell you how to do it. | True | False |

The questionnaires laid out on pages 22 and 23 are example templates that you can adopt and adapt for use with your own pupils.

The request for the children to circle 'true' or 'false' was a conscious decision on our part, as young children naturally see ticks and crosses as symbols for *correct* or *incorrect*. As an NQT, Julia learnt this after writing her end of year reports. The day after receiving her son's report, a parent came in to explain how upset her child had been at the grid in the report which shows effort and attainment. Julia had been instructed to put a cross in the column which best indicated how much effort had been put in (unsatisfactory, satisfactory, good or excellent). The little boy had seen a table full of crosses and became convinced that it meant he'd got all the subjects wrong. Julia has always remembered the connection he made, and has used dots from then on – a tick might have been interpreted in the same confused way, although in the inverse: positively.

It is important that the children don't feel as though we are looking for 'correctness' in their answers – we want them to answer honestly, without regard to getting something right for the teacher. A child who answers the green questions with 'true' might have a natural propensity towards a growth mindset; while a child who answers the blue questions with 'true' is likely to have a naturally more fixed mindset.

The answers your pupils give will shed a surprising amount of light on how they view learning. They might surprise you with unexpected responses, which shows how important it is for you to know and understand your pupils' mindsets. It can be quite sad to discover that certain bright, happy pupils have such a fixed mindset, attributing success and pleasure purely to getting answers correct. Likewise, children whose answers show a calm and happy attitude to learning and challenge will light up your teaching fire. It's when all children are heading in that direction together that our classrooms become raging furnaces of learning – with motivated children who are skilled at accepting and welcoming new challenges.

For our youngest children, a questionnaire would, of course, be useless. We need a reasonable way to get an insight into how their mindsets are forming. This will be wholly influenced by their home and family experiences prior to starting in your setting. It is the only stage on which they've played out their life so far. Their learning has consisted of playing and growing, noticing the world around them and imitating their parents and siblings. With that in mind, we can see how parents' mindsets might influence children who are new to education and to school- or nursery-based learning. Fabian and Dunlop mention the importance of this phase:

> children move from 'child in the family' to 'pupil in the school' and [...] the values of home and school often differ. These include differences in the way in which play at home and play at school is perceived according to family and cultural values, and may cause emotional difficulties for children.[1]

The best way to create a little window into their world is by watching them at play and listening to them communicate. We have to hold ourselves back and try to spot what they show us independently. It's amazing how much information a three-year-old can provide when you sit back and watch. A lot more than a questionnaire will give you, we'd like to bet!

If you have children in your care who are able communicators and who like to join in by sharing their own thoughts and ideas, then stories are another way with which to gauge how children's mindsets are forming. Through good-quality questioning and interaction with a story, children will happily share their feelings and ideas, from which you can judge both their readiness to start engaging with growth mindset ideas and how their mindsets are orientated on the fixed–growth spectrum.

To help support your observations (or 'episodes of watching', as we like to say – we have far too many observations in our lives already), the short prompt paper that follows might help. It links directly to the characteristics of effective learning from the government-issued *Early Years Foundation Stage Profile*.[2] The characteristics of effective learning are learning behaviours that early years teachers are expected to foster in their pupils. They form part of assessments in this phase, and pupils' progress in demonstrating these behaviours is reported to parents. It's also nice to keep a record so you can look back when you come to the end of your endeavour and see just how far that little learner has come. You can make a mark next to the behaviours that are demonstrated, and add examples in the relevant columns.

---

1   Hilary Fabian and Aline-Wendy Dunlop, *Outcomes of Good Practice in Transition Processes for Children Entering Primary School*. Working Paper 42 (The Hague: Bernard van Leer Foundation, 2007), p. 6.
2   Standards and Testing Agency, *Early Years Foundation Stage Profile: 2019 Handbook*. Ref: STA/19/8311/e (10 December 2018). Available at: https://www.gov.uk/government/publications/early-years-foundation-stage-profile-handbook. The characteristics of effective learning are detailed on p. 22.

| Child's name:<br>Date:<br>Episode of watching to focus on mindset. Number of minutes: | What the child says: | What the child does: |
|---|---|---|
| Growth mindset demonstrated by:<br><br>Approaching a new task happily ___<br><br>Keeping on trying even when things get tough ___<br><br>Trying another way when one attempt doesn't work ___<br><br>Demonstrating a willingness to 'have a go' ___<br><br>Watching someone else and then trying out what they did ___<br><br>Enjoying the activity for the pleasure of it, rather than the end result ___<br><br>Remaining calm and happy even when things go wrong ___ | | |
| Fixed mindset demonstrated by:<br><br>Giving up when something is tricky ___ | | |

| | | |
|---|---|---|
| Not even attempting something that looks tricky \_\_\_ | | |
| Trying something the same way over and over again, even if it doesn't work \_\_\_ | | |
| Bringing things to show you that aren't their best efforts \_\_\_ | | |
| Leaving an activity unfinished \_\_\_ | | |
| Asking another child to do something for them rather than trying to do it themselves \_\_\_ | | |

Episode of watching prompt paper

# MINDSET MINI STORIES

We mentioned the value of using stories to explore the mindsets of younger learners. We created these mini stories as a tool to see into pupils' reasoning in situations in which mindset has a part to play. They are simple stories that present scenarios which are very familiar to children – play and learning activities – and they'll have the opportunity to discuss them with you. They might tell of similar situations that they've been in or give an opinion about what is happening to the characters. They act as a simple springboard into a discussion between you and the pupils, which will be valuable and insightful, even at the simplest level. Where a word is underlined, there is a picture to accompany it, which can be downloaded from www.crownhouse.co.uk/featured/learning-without-fear.

## Mini story 1

I'm going to tell you about Anna. She loves going to school. Every morning she runs in after giving her big brother a kiss goodbye. She always runs straight for the sand area, as she loves how it feels in her hands. One morning, Anna came in as usual, but the sand tray had disappeared! Where could it have gone, she wondered. Mr Clarke, the teacher, noticed that Anna seemed worried. He asked Anna what was wrong. 'I only want to play in the sand,' Anna replied, a tear rolling down her cheek. What do you think Anna could do? What do you think Mr Clarke will do?

Prompts:

Do you like coming into school like Anna does?

Do you have a favourite thing to do? Why is it your favourite?

Was Anna right to cry? Why? Why not?

Why do you think we put out different things to do each week/day?

Is it okay that the sand has gone? Why? Why not?

What do you do when you first come into school?

What would you do if you were Anna?

What should Mr Clarke do?

## Mini story 2

Harry is three years old. He doesn't like balancing an egg on a spoon. It's tricky, but he's seen Anjali do it and run at the same time! One morning in nursery, Harry sat and watched Anjali with her egg and spoon. She did it a bit differently to Harry. She held out her arm straight and solid, which helped her keep the egg balanced. Harry copied Anjali and managed to balance his egg for five seconds! He asked Anjali to play with him, and she showed him how to run slowly with the egg still balanced. They had wonderful fun, and Harry got even better with a little bit of practice.

Prompts:

Why doesn't Harry like balancing the egg?

What gives him some ideas to try to make him a bit better at it?

Would you like to try balancing an egg on a spoon? Why? Why not?

Have you ever watched someone to see how to do something?

How can our friends help us?

What will Anjali's teacher say to her?

How long do you think Harry will balance it for after lots of practice?

What will Harry's teacher say to him?

## Mini story 3

In Mrs Jones' class, there is a little boy called <u>Ali</u>. Ali loves Mrs Jones. He always wants to show her his models and paintings. When he shows her, she says, 'Well done!' and 'What a clever boy!' Ali feels good when she says these things to him. One morning, Mrs Jones looked at a model that Ali had made. It was a <u>tower of blocks that looked a bit like a castle</u>. Mrs Jones looked at the model and said, 'Ali, I think you can make that even better ...' Ali was surprised. 'Why didn't she like it?' he thought to himself. He felt a bit upset. Mrs Jones noticed that Ali was a bit sad. She sat with him and helped him to think of ways he could make the tower look even more like a castle. Together, they thought of some super ideas, like <u>finding some different-shaped blocks to make turrets</u>. By the time they'd finished, Ali was even more proud of himself. They took a photo and put it up on the wall. The display was called 'Our Best Work'.

Prompts:

Was Ali's model extra special at first? Why? Why not?

Would you like to build something with your teacher? Why? Why not?

Have you ever done something that could have been even better if you'd done your best work?

Why was Ali a bit sad after showing Mrs Jones the tower?

What will Ali do with the blocks the next day in school?

Why does Ali like showing his work to Mrs Jones?

What might Ali tell his family when he gets home from school?

Can you describe Ali's castle after he'd made it better?

## Mini story 4

On her first day of nursery, three-year-old Ellie found an easel with paints next to it. She could see her name on her peg from where she stood. She had an idea. She would try to write her name in paint using her finger. She dipped her finger in the paint. Slowly, she tried to make the letter 'E' for Ellie. It looked a bit wonky. Next, she tried to do the 'l'. It went wobbly and long! Her teacher, Mr Betts, came to see what she was painting. He thought it was great that she was painting letters and sounds. He said to Ellie, 'What have you written?' Ellie was cross. 'He should know!' she thought. She decided to try again on a new piece of paper. This time he will know, she thought. Her 'E' was a little less wonky. Her 'l' looked a bit straighter. Mr Betts noticed she was trying again. He looked and could see the letters more clearly. This time, Ellie was proud. Mr Betts said, 'It's super that you tried again, Ellie. Practice makes perfect!' By the time she was four, Ellie's finger-painted name looked even better.

Prompts:

Why did Ellie choose to paint the letters of her name?

Why do you think that her first try was a bit wonky and wobbly?

Why was Ellie cross?

Have you ever practised something?

What else could Ellie practise in school?

How do you get better at writing letters?

What might Mr Betts have said to Ellie's mum that day?

## Mini story 5

<u>Majus</u> loves cars. He doesn't speak much English, but he can understand some things that the children in his class say to him. He speaks Polish at home. Majus' nursery class were busy getting ready for an assembly. All the parents would be there. Miss Lees helped Majus to build a <u>model of his favourite car</u> out of construction bricks. She asked him to show it during the assembly. Majus started crying and shaking his head. <u>He felt scared</u>. His friend, Tomasz, put his arm round Majus and encouraged him. Miss Lees helped Majus feel a bit better. They practised a few more times, and Majus started to feel a bit excited. He knew he would be proud of himself if he was brave. It was a challenge! That Friday, he showed his model in the assembly. His mum clapped very hard at the end. She knew that Majus found it hard, but <u>he did it</u>!

Prompts:

Why do you think Majus started to feel excited about showing his car after a while?

How did Majus feel about the assembly at first?

How did Miss Lees help him?

What did his mum feel?

What did he feel when they did the assembly for the parents?

Do you think Majus would like to do another assembly? Why? Why not?

If your pupils begin to demonstrate an understanding of the situations in the mini stories, you could try reading picture books which relate to mindset and exploring some of the feelings involved. You'll find a list of recommendations in the references and further reading section at the back of the book. We've suggested these as they are a good source of inspiration for further work, and some are discussed in greater detail in Chapter 10, in which we explore lesson ideas.

Chapter 3
# TEACHING SUCCESS

Time for another visualisation. Imagine that you are about to climb a small peak somewhere in the UK. You may have already done this, in which case draw on that experience. Ruchi hasn't climbed a mountain before (this is part of a fixed mindset about hiking – she's working on it!) but she imagines that the feelings before and during are similar to those we might have when faced with other challenging life experiences – such as going for a promotion, dealing with a change in personal circumstances, starting a new job and not fully knowing the expectations yet, and so on.

You are climbing the hillside at a steady speed. The air is crisp, and you are enjoying the opportunity to take it at your own pace. After a couple of hours of steady climbing, the path narrows to traverse a very narrow crest, only a metre wide in some places. You are suddenly very aware of how high up you are and you start to feel the tiniest wave of anxiety. Beads of sweat build on your forehead as you realise that the only way forward is following the exposed path ahead. The wind whips around you and that anxiety wave is slowly starting to ripple. Rationally, you know that it is safe, and that thousands of people have done it before you; this shouldn't be a problem. But still, you can't deny the fear as you're faced with the increasingly difficult task ahead of you. You know you only have two options: you can either admit defeat and go back down the way you came, unsuccessful and unfulfilled, or you can face the feelings of dread, push yourself physically and mentally and carry on to successful completion.

Now we want you to think carefully about what specific behaviours or skills will help you to succeed in the face of difficulty. What will push you out of your comfort zone and over that mountain? Consider the kind of traits that can be applied to any setback or obstacle in order to overcome it.

We have delivered lots of training on growth mindset and we often ask the audience this question right at the beginning. No matter the group, when we go around the room and gather responses there are always the same set of answers, which we have laid out in the grid that follows.

| determination | perseverance | confidence | resilience | teamwork | bravery |
|---|---|---|---|---|---|
| conviction | self-belief | tenacity | practice | boldness | self-regulation |
| fortitude | patience | mindfulness | ambition | optimism | drive |
| strength of will | instinct | courage | initiative | creative thinking | positivity |

As adults, we often have to utilise these qualities at work and in our personal lives. Experience has taught us to use them almost instinctively in times of great need. What's even more interesting is that no one has ever offered up 'intelligence' as an attribute to draw on in the face of struggle. Being clever is not necessarily conducive to success. Which begs the question, if the skills listed here are those that we seem to universally accept as providing the key to success, why are we not explicitly teaching them in lessons?

Let's bring it back to your classroom. No matter what age group you teach, we want you to mentally fast forward to the end of the academic year. What kind of learners do you want to see? What are they going to be like after your specific input? Are they going to climb the mountain or turn back because of self-doubt and fear? As obvious as it may seem, *you* hold the power and influence to make the changes you want to see in the minds of the pupils you teach. It really is as simple as that. We know; it's a huge privilege, but what a responsibility! Professor John Hattie bravely admitted what the profession has secretly always known, that it's the teach*er* that makes the real difference in the classroom, not the teach*ing*. As he said in a speech at a researchEd conference in Melbourne, 'I could not care less about how you teach! I care about the impact of your teaching and about how you think about your teaching.'[1] What *you* believe and how you convey it will transfer directly to your pupils. In the classroom, you are the parent, guide and master and it really is no exaggeration when we say that everything you say and do has impact. To quote Spiderman's Uncle Ben, 'With great power comes great responsibility.'

---

1    John Hattie, 'I could not care less about how you teach!' Speech given at researchEd conference, Melbourne, 1 July 2017. Video available at: https://visible-learning.org/2017/08/john-hattie-how-you-teach-video/.

While you recover from the gravity of that, let us highlight the beliefs about learning that we should instil in our pupils. As well as the traits listed previously, these will form the foundations of their growth mindset:

| | | |
|---|---|---|
| Higher-order critical thinking | Autonomy | Valuing hard work |
| Conviction to manage tough decisions | | Pace and patience |
| Bouncebackability | Effective self-reflection and assessment | Initiative and audacity |
| Openness to challenge | Readiness to collaborate | Self-belief |
| Effort | Willingness to seek help | Resilience to setbacks |
| Sound practical judgement | Boldness of enterprise | Determination and tenacity |

There is a subtle but powerful variance between failing and failure. We need to help our pupils understand how failing is not a definition of their ability and does not determine their future outcomes. *Failing* is turning back down that mountain, maybe to try the climb again under different conditions, or with better resources. *Failure* is never climbing a mountain again and the difference, of course, is in how many of these traits have been internalised as part of your mindset.

| Failing | Being a failure |
|---|---|
| An event | A mindset |
| Temporary | Permanent |

| Failing | Being a failure |
|---|---|
| Shows that you stretch the limits | Shows that you gave up |
| An opportunity to learn | The end of learning |

Self-determinism is a theory that delves further into this area and although on the surface it might sound rather academic, it's actually a very sound and important idea for teaching mindset. We'd recommend reading further if you are interested in this area of research.[2] We could go on but, in the interest of time and word count, we shall summarise. Self-determinism assumes that humans are intrinsically predisposed to be curious about our environment; we are driven to learn and to develop knowledge, which pretty much summarises how very young children approach any task (early years colleagues will back us up here).

Unfortunately, within the constrictions of the curriculum – and the imposed assessment structure determining what children must learn by particular ages – this natural state is quashed by educators who impose external controls onto learning environments, which can undermine the sense of *relatedness* between teachers and pupils. All too often, these controls can stifle the natural processes involved in high-quality learning. Conversely, we've found that when we support learners' basic psychological needs for relatedness, autonomy and competence, it helps to create pupils who are independent in their learning, and who take responsibility for what they are achieving. It's what we all aim for as teachers. This fits in neatly with what we've been talking about in terms of mindset; if we get these three factors right in our classrooms, we've essentially got the perfect recipe for nurturing intrinsically motivated learners. Easy, right?

---

2   For a good starting point, try Edward L. Deci with Richard Flaste, *Why We Do What We Do: Understanding Self-Motivation* (London: Penguin, 1996); and Richard M. Ryan and Edward L. Deci, Self-Determination Theory and the Facilitation of Intrinsic Motivation, Social Development, and Well-Being, *American Psychologist*, 55(1) (2000): 68–78.

# THE FEAR

We all experience the fear: at home, at work, in conversation with colleagues, around the table at dinner parties, in the classroom when a child asks us a question we just don't know the answer to but feel as though we *should* (particularly when another adult is watching – even worse when it's a spelling or calculation question). So where does this come from? At what point do we start to feel self-conscious, worried or *scared* when answering questions? Where does this fear of 'looking stupid' come from?

At a #LearningFirst conference at the University of Cumbria in November 2016, Ruchi heard a colleague speak about this feeling, and she articulated it very well. She was talking about questioning and she asked the audience of teachers to turn to one another and imagine that they had asked a fairly routine maths question. Next, she asked us to imagine that we had chosen a child to answer and that they had come out with the most random, bonkers response ever heard (we've all been there). We dutifully complied, and it resulted in 200 teachers showing each other faces that were a mixture of confused, irritated and disappointed (and in some cases a bit cross). Some seemed pitiful or patronising and some (unsuccessfully) tried to stifle a smile. Try it yourself in the mirror or with a colleague, you might be surprised at what you see.

Then she said the thing that hit Ruchi right in the ribs, so brace yourselves. The face that we could see looking back at us – the irritated, bemused one – is the face our pupils see when they say something that isn't right or that doesn't equate with what we were expecting. *That* is the face that makes children feel stupid. We can have the best intentions in the world, we can think we are giving the most inclusive, encouraging feedback, but, in the end, children are incredibly perceptive, particularly with non-verbal cues. They can see when they have let us down by being 'wrong' or because they haven't been able to guess what was in our heads. Some of our pupils might never recover from the one time it happened and that is what triggers the fear. That is precisely what we need to eradicate. We've got some work to do.

What we need in bucketfuls is courage. How are you going to make your pupils braver? How will you get them to the point where they are not afraid to be curious, to ask questions and to try things out? How can we make them feel safe? Ruchi's colleague at the conference suggested that questioning played a key role, with the aim of not having anything in your head that your pupils are trying to guess at – more on that when we look at questioning in Chapter 6. However, we think our work starts earlier than that.

We need to grasp the idea that, in the classroom, we are all in it together and there is safety in numbers: what we refer to as *relatedness*. The fear is not a rational thought process, it is an unwanted feeling that creeps into our learner psyche and can sometimes feel crippling. Your pupils need to feel supported to learn by everyone in the space in order to counter it. The classroom needs to become a safe space – one where you will firmly close, lock and bolt the door behind you in order to keep the fear out.

Feeling safe to discuss, perform, question and share in the classroom is a rejection of the fear that prevents us from stepping out of our comfort zone and into the realm of challenge and learning.[3] A simple discussion is a great way to start building this idea straight away and can easily form the basis of a whole day of learning around bravery and courage (which we will explore as the lesson idea Safe Classroom, see pages 56–58).

We often talk about the fear in maths because most children can relate to this feeling easily – it's typical to feel fixed in this subject. When we are scared about being wrong, irrational or self-hindering thoughts creep into our psyche and it renders us immobile and, in some cases, speechless.

---

3   This is based on Lev Vygotsky's work on the Zones of Proximal Development (ZPD), defined as the difference between what a learner can do without help and what they can't do. See Lev Vygotsky, Interaction Between Learning and Development. In Mary Gauvain and Michael Cole (eds), *Readings on the Development of Children* (New York: Scientific American Books, 1978), pp. 34–40. Available at: https://www.faculty.mun.ca/cmattatall/Vygotsky_1978.pdf.

What will my
teacher think of
me if I don't know?

They're all going
to find out that
I don't know, and I
won't look clever.

What if everyone
laughs at me?

I think I know the
answer, but it's too
obvious - this must be
a trick.

I feel sick!

What if I'm wrong?

This is where the idea of the safe classroom comes into play. You need to explore these thoughts explicitly and talk about the feelings of nervousness and panic that arise when we are put on the spot. In a safe classroom, those feelings of fear don't exist because all ideas, answers, voices and opinions are heard and valued. Although we might disagree or think that an idea needs a bit of work, as a team, we talk about it openly, feel comfortable to challenge others without shaming them and understand that there is more than one way of looking at something. You will find that, over time, when we ask the pupils to explain why they agree or disagree and bounce it back to them, their respect for each other naturally grows. Your role is crucial to this process because you will need to model the language and behaviour involved every time you engage with the whole class. Consistently bring them back into the safe classroom through your modelling. Perhaps you could even create a safe display so that you can point the children towards it every time you sense hesitation in sharing ideas.

The key is to align everyone in the class to this concept; it's safe for everyone, including the adults. The pupils need to believe that the classroom is their space to ask questions, explore, invent, investigate, challenge and cooperate. When we take the idea of competition out of the equation, children (and adults) stop measuring their successes against others' and begin to understand the value of difference and individuality.

In *Time to Think* Nancy Kline outlines ten key components of a thinking environment, which we think underpin everything we value when it comes to creating a classroom of relatedness.[4] By this we mean a classroom in which pupils feel supported and connected to their teacher and to each other, particularly when facing challenge or difficulty. Studies into relatedness show that when learning communities are united by positive feelings of connection, empathy and support, this improves outcomes.[5]

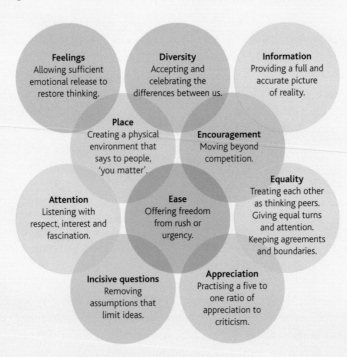

4   Nancy Kline, *Time to Think: Listening to Ignite the Human Mind* (London: Octopus Books, 1999), p. 35.
5   For example, Richard M. Ryan and Cynthia L. Powelson, Autonomy and Relatedness as Fundamental to Motivation and Education, *The Journal of Experimental Education*, 60(1) (1991): 49–66; and Amori Yee Mikami, Erik A. Ruzek, Christopher A. Hafen, Anne Gregory and Joseph P. Allen, Perceptions of Relatedness with Classroom Peers Promote Adolescents' Behavioral Engagement and Achievement in Secondary School, *Journal of Youth and Adolescence*, 46(11) (2017): 2341–2354.

By adopting just a few of these principles into the routines and language of your classroom you will start to notice a shift in the way your pupils interact with each other. The key is to provide the opportunities for these principles to play out easily.

# FROM STUCK ISLAND TO GOT-IT CITY VIA CHALLENGE OCEAN

Okay, you've got your pupils talking and listening, and hopefully their confidence is starting to increase and they are relating to each other, so what's next? Well, it's time to make the learning journey and the struggle that comes with it explicit; they need some experiences and feelings to relate to. Time for a little story now – get your goggles on, we're diving into another analogy.

Imagine you are sitting on a beach, the sand is soft and golden, the air is warm but comfortable and the speckled sunshine is beating down gloriously on your back. You can hear the gentle lapping of the ocean waves as you settle down for a lazy mid-afternoon nap. Just as you are about to drift off you catch yourself thinking, 'This is paradise. I could stay here forever.'

But we all know what happens when you have too much of a good thing. What starts out wonderfully can quickly turn sour, and it's no different here on Stuck Island. You see, this is the place that feels comfortable at first – you know everything about the island, there's nothing new or difficult to worry about. There are no obstacles and you know exactly what to expect. The trouble is, very quickly, you start to realise that Stuck Island is kind of boring. There's nothing to do – except all the activities you've already done repeatedly – the sun is far too strong and everyone else on the island is leaving to make their way towards something new. When you look out at the horizon you can see the bright lights of Got-It City – a vibrant and exciting place full of possibility, wonder and endless opportunities. Slowly but surely, you accept that, as easy as it is to stay on the island, you need to leave. The warm fuzziness you once felt is starting to burn. 'I'm going for it,' you say to yourself. 'I'm going to get myself to Got-It City.'

If only it were that simple. You see, there is something vast and scary in-between where you are and where you want to go. Something that scares you so much, you start to convince yourself that Stuck Island isn't so bad after all. Sure, it's the same thing day in, day out, you've learnt to make every type of sandcastle imaginable, and you're lonely and mind-numbingly fed up, but the thought of leaving fills you with a feeling that is far worse. The fear has taken over, for in front of you lies Challenge Ocean, a dangerous and daunting stretch of water, full of potential dangers and difficulties.

'I'm not a confident swimmer, there's no way I can do it,' you say to yourself. You start to reel off a list of objections and worries:

It'll take too long.

It's too much effort.

I'm not good enough.

The current is too strong.

I don't have enough energy.

I don't know the way.

It's too far away.

There are sharks in there.

What if I drown?

What if I get lost?

What if I can't stay afloat?

I'm scared.

I'm fine exactly where I am.

No, you conclude, it's best to stay where you are, safe among what you know and without obvious difficulties. How you feel on Stuck Island is exactly how it feels when you realise it's time to try something different and more demanding. You know you should, and you do want to. But what's familiar is also very comfortable, and crossing over into unknown waters is an open invitation for the fear to creep in. This is an analogy we have often used with pupils: the concept of Stuck Island is an accessible symbol of the fear stifling our learning.

Our classes have really run with this metaphor and find that they can relate to the idea of being stuck in quicksand and feeling unable to keep going. Pupils have likened this to learning moments in which they have not been able to move forward with a tricky problem, so have either given up or gone backwards and attempted tasks which they knew they could already do. 'It's not really learning if you can already do it,' one pupil offered wisely. The analogy also works to unpick why it might be worse to stay on the island rather than take the plunge and dive into the water. In class we have talked about how the island will eventually take hold of you and make you feel as though you can't leave: there are crabs pinching at your toes as you edge closer to Challenge Ocean and quicksand that drags you down and stops you reaching your full potential. Feeling as though you can't do something really does hurt! It's painful to realise that you are not able to participate in something that seems to come easily to your peers. In a safe classroom it's important to explore and openly discuss these feelings of inferiority.

The more these feelings are normalised, the more your pupils will learn to ignore and overcome them.

On the other side of Challenge Ocean is the buzz of Got-It City: the place where everyone can thrive and where the fear disappears. The city is the opposite of Stuck Island. Everything is new, exciting and open to possibility. When pupils arrive here, they can feel proud that they have overcome their challenges, completed a difficult task, solved a problem or finally grasped a concept that has been puzzling them for a while. The feelings of accomplishment you get from reaching it are to be celebrated and, crucially, children should be encouraged to talk about how they got there. It's important for them to accept that the waters of Challenge Ocean are not smooth and that if they were, perhaps it wasn't really a challenge after all.

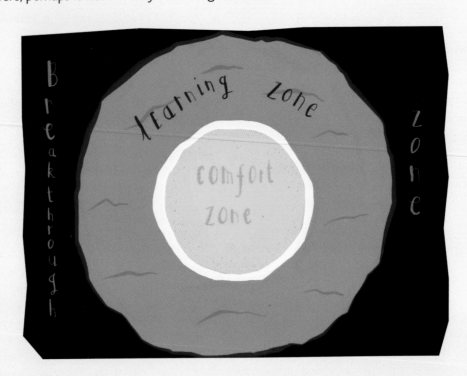

You might have encountered the learning zone model before.[6] The concept suggests that, in learning situations, the moment we step out of what is comfortable and into unknown territory – terrain which is scary and demanding – is when learning happens. It's one of the most exciting places to be and, as teachers, we must provide as many opportunities as possible for pupils to experience the learning zone. In our model, Challenge Ocean is the learning zone and Got-It City is the breakthrough zone.

## Challenge Ocean

Remember when we were on that mountain earlier and had to face the fear that made us want to turn back? Remember those feelings of doubt and discomfort that you have to push through in order to reach a goal? This is all that Challenge Ocean represents. Trying to swim in it is the fear personified and all those niggling doubts can be hard to ignore with the vast expanse of the ocean in front of you. In a safe classroom, pupils can liken difficult questions or tasks to swimming in Challenge Ocean. It's going to take effort and time and, more importantly, you're probably going to need some tools to help you. This is where the handy survival kit comes into play (see page 48). Our pupils really enjoy using this kit as a reference point for how to get themselves unstuck.

Each tool in the kit has been included to reinforce the traits we discussed earlier in this chapter: resourcefulness, collaboration, self-regulation, creativity, patience and a willingness to seek help, and also to encourage pupils to use the scaffolds we provide – for example, success criteria. Interestingly, our pupils love the idea of using the snorkel, because sometimes we just need to take a moment to breathe! It's okay if that times table doesn't come to us straight away; if we allow ourselves time to think, to take a breath and to remember not to let the fear take over, the answer soon comes. We have also used props to reinforce these ideas, sometimes bringing the items into class or even spending time making our own. Children love putting on the goggles when checking their work or pretending to light the flare when they want some teacher feedback.

---

6   A good summary can be found at: http://www.thempra.org.uk/social-pedagogy/key-concepts-in-social-pedagogy/the-learning-zone-model/. The original work by Tom Senninger (*Abenteuer leiten, in Abenteuern learnen* (Münster: Ökotopia Verlag, 2000)) is, unfortunately, not available in English.

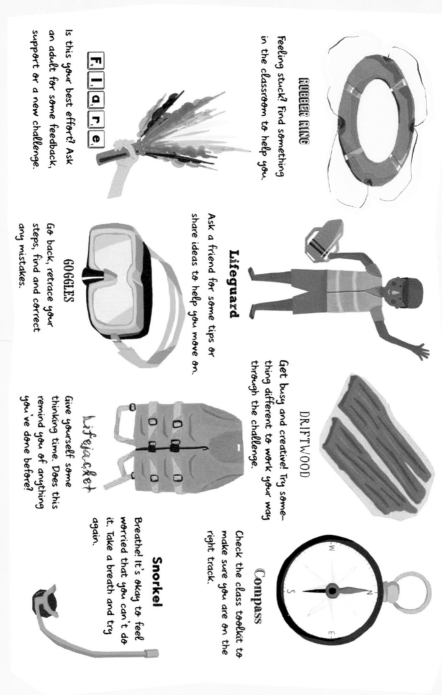

## RUBBER RING

Feeling stuck? Find something in the classroom to help you.

## F.l.a.r.e.

Is this your best effort? Ask an adult for some feedback, support or a new challenge.

## Lifeguard

Ask a friend for some tips or share ideas to help you move on.

## GOGGLES

Go back, retrace your steps, find and correct any mistakes.

## DRIFTWOOD

Get busy and creative! Try something different to work your way through the challenge.

## Lifejacket

Give yourself some thinking time. Does this remind you of anything you've done before?

## Compass

Check the class toolkit to make sure you are on the right track.

## Snorkel

Breathe! It's okay to feel worried that you can't do it. Take a breath and try again.

48

The survival kit has been designed to remind pupils to take ownership in the face of struggle and to use metacognitive devices to reinforce their self-regulation within a learning task. Too often we have sat in lessons in which pupils sit with their hands up, waiting for an adult to tell them what to do or to hand them a resource. Sometimes those with fixed mindsets don't even ask because of the fear, and this just isn't good enough. We are simply not equipping our pupils with the independence they require in order to succeed beyond primary school. As Yates states:

> Students with learned helplessness see success as determined by factors such as luck which are outside of their control (Seligman, 1993). Furthermore, they generally believe they will never be successful at school for a variety of reasons including their perceived lack of ability (Dweck & Repucci, 1973) and the difficulty of the tasks.[7]

Remember the three basic needs that self-determinism informs us about: relatedness, autonomy and competence? We need to begin with the culture of relatedness in the classroom, then provide the right environment in which to explore autonomy and freedom and, finally, offer enough guidance and input to develop the pupils' competency in any task. The survival kit is a way to make this visible and user-friendly for your pupils and can help to create a common language of learning in your classroom. We'd recommend having the survival kit displayed prominently, and making reference to the tools regularly. It's a great idea to ask pupils which bits of the kit they think they might need before they start a task and then to reflect on what they did use at the end. Guide them to reflect on whether and how the tools were useful and whether they would recommend them to a partner. Every child has the potential to be a lifeguard in any skill or subject area – to help others if they are struggling. This reinforces the belief that we can learn from each other, no matter how fixed our ideas about our own 'abilities' are. If a pupil has swam the length of Challenge Ocean and made it to Got-It City, they can be celebrated as a lifeguard in whatever skill they were working on, helping them to further master their skillset and giving them the confidence to try things they may have previously avoided.

---

7    Shirley Yates, Teacher Identification of Student Learned Helplessness in Mathematics, *Mathematics Education Research Journal*, 21(3) (2009): 86–106 at 87.

Professor Barry Hymer has co-authored some useful books on mindset and has sum-marised what it might look like in learning tasks.[8] This links in wonderfully with the idea of learner self-regulation and metacognition that we will look at in Chapter 5. In short, the cycle of metacognitive learning and mindset revolves around an awareness of what we do and don't know, and our understanding that improving what we know involves an active process of recognising, regulating and manipulating our cognitive processes.

---

8   Pete Boyd, Barry Hymer and Karen Lockney, *Learning Teaching: Becoming an Inspirational Teacher* (Northwich: Critical Publishing, 2015); and Barry Hymer and Mike Gershon, *Growth Mindset Pocketbook* (Alresford: Teachers' Pocketbooks, 2014).

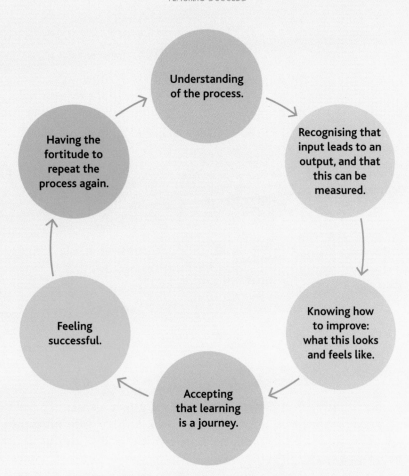

Once your pupils are on board with the idea of Challenge Ocean you can start to explore what might happen when you go for a swim. Before the ideas are embedded, children focus on the setbacks they may face – encountering sharks, for instance. What's wonderful about the concept of the ocean is that you can start having meaningful conversations about surface and deep learning.

When our understanding is at surface level – meaning that we haven't explored the task, skill or problem in any great detail – we may think we have understood the subject matter really well. However, there may be more below that surface. The same can be true when we face a problem. On the surface it can appear unsolvable, but if we scratch the surface and use our tools to help us go deeper, we find that things aren't as scary as we might have thought. Jump into the difficulty feet first and you might find that what looked like sharks are actually friendly dolphins, and no one wants to miss out on swimming with dolphins.

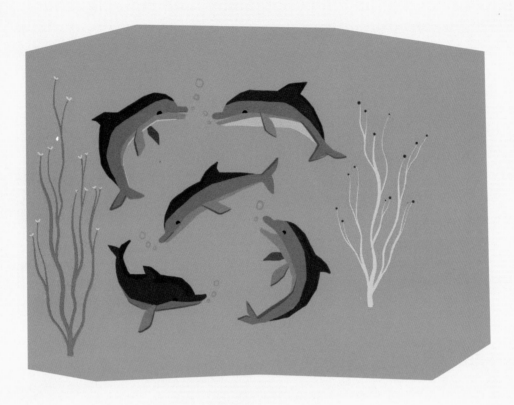

As soon as we dip our toes into a challenge, what seemed scary might not be after all. Once we overcome obstacles on our learning journey and give ourselves time to reflect on our success, we often realise that the fear is what skews our perception. Depth of understanding comes when we overcome the fear, and it opens up a whole world of wonder. Wouldn't it be incredible to have a class full of children who were curious and excited about diving deep into their learning? In Chapter 10 we outline a series of lesson ideas which detail how to extend and explore the Stuck Island analogy with the children.

## SO WHAT DOES THIS MEAN IN *YOUR* CLASSROOM?

John Hattie's synthesis of meta-analyses – the culmination of 15 years of research – concluded that explicit teaching about metacognition and mindset can have the biggest impact on learning when it is taught through the principle of self-determinism.[9] When we have those three core ideas – relatedness, autonomy and competence – at the heart of our teaching, we provide the right environment for success.

When we talk about learning environments, we are not just referring to physical features like layout or displays. It is the all-important culture of the classroom that really matters: the shared values, priorities, expectations, language, habits and routines. However,

---

9    John Hattie, *Visible Learning: A Synthesis of Over 800 Meta-Analyses Relating to Achievement* (Abingdon and New York: Routledge, 2009).

working walls and displays do play an important role in the function of your classroom and we shouldn't underestimate these as a powerful tool for cultivating change. Even if your school culture is not in line with your own ideas of what it could or should be, believe us when we say that great things can come from small changes. This might be the hardest job of all in terms of mindset change, but you need to believe that you can be the change you want to see. Don't wait for senior management to green-flag your ideas; be brave and try them out for yourself.

In order to change the culture of a setting, you need to scale back and start with the *climate* to facilitate a shift in thinking, language, interactions, relationships, actions and, ultimately, mindset. In teaching, we are regularly presented with opportunities to invite change in our classrooms. Each half term provides us with, essentially, a blank canvas, as we continually seek to improve our practice and refine our approaches. Strategies that didn't work last time can be scrapped in favour of shiny new ideas and initiatives. We are incredibly lucky in our profession; we can't think of another job in which you can refresh and reinvent your working space so easily and frequently. We urge you to grab these incredible opportunities throughout your teaching career, to read about and research strategies that might work for you and to have the courage to implement them in your classroom.

# LESSON IDEAS

If you'd like to start putting these principles into practice, here is a lesson idea, which is a taster of what you'll find in Chapter 10 (the icon key is on page 180). It aims to start building the children's acceptance of feeling uncomfortable – to show them that they can feel safe in answering questions and approaching new tasks.

## Safe Classroom

### Intention(s)

To scaffold the pupils' thinking and encourage them to share their ideas freely. In this task, the teacher will ask questions, listen to all groups and pick out key themes in order to guide the learning. To help pupils to understand the feelings of discomfort we experience when fear stifles our curiosity. To introduce the idea of a safe classroom, where all ideas, thoughts and answers are valued.

### Resources

A picture of a safe on the interactive whiteboard or placed on tables.

A flipchart.

### Activity

As a quick warm-up, show the children a picture of a safe and ask them to individually jot down all the things they know it could be used for – this could be on a mini-whiteboard or in their books. Share some suggestions and take notes.

Next, ask the children to pair up and think about what makes them feel safe. Ask them to discuss this then share ideas as a class. Depending on the age of the children, you could ask them how the classroom is a safe place. Generally, we have found that most children tend to go for the obvious ideas: kind adults, locked doors, school gates (we even had someone suggest CCTV one year), but the key is to guide them to think beyond the tangible components of 'safety' and towards those abstract fuzzy feelings of comfort and a sense of well-being.

Next, show the pupils a series of images chosen to evoke specific feelings of comfort or discomfort. Ask them to write down one word associated with each image. Then ask them what they fear the most and record the answers as they are shared. Ask a handful of pupils what they do to try to overcome their fear and who helps them to achieve this.

In groups, ask pupils to discuss what they fear the most when they are in class. They need to come up with one main idea to share.

A range of pictures to induce feelings of comfort/discomfort, including a difficult maths problem. Examples could include: a spider, a family, a roller coaster, a cute puppy, an assault course, a happy classroom, etc.

A device you can use to play a YouTube clip.

Using the pupils' answers to steer the learning, go back to the maths calculation image and pick this one apart. Without any specific answers in mind, ask the following:

- What do you see?
- How is this connected to what we have been talking about?
- How does the picture make you feel?
- Imagine if I asked you to give me the answer, how would you feel then?
- What's the worst thing that could happen if you are wrong?
- What might I do or say?
- What might the other children do or say?

Pupils generally assume that the worst thing that could happen is that everyone else will laugh. It's worth building on this point to talk about whether this has actually happened to anyone and whether it is likely to. Build a scale of likeliness, with positive outcomes at the top and negative ones at the bottom. Add this to the class working wall.

Ask pupils to contribute ideas for a class manifesto on keeping the classroom safe from the fear. Compile it together and display it at the front of the room.

If you need a little inspiration, there is a great video which you could watch to generate a conversation about facing our learning fears and celebrating bravery.[10] Decide how this will be positively

---

10  Soul Pancake, 'Kid President Presents the Scariest Thing in the World' [video] (27 October 2016). Available at: https://www.youtube.com/watch?v=x9SwbLN-OvY&index=3&list=PLzvRx_johoA-YabI6FWcU-jL6nKA1Um-t.

reinforced in the classroom – with a thumbs up, a nomination for best fear-facer at the end of the day, etc.

Ask the pupils to draw a visual representation of the fear. They can screw it up into a ball and then throw it away (but you could unfurl the drawings and use them as part of a safe classroom display).

## Chapter 4

# LEARNING ENVIRONMENTS AND DISPLAYS

When you walk into a classroom, it's often very easy to gauge the teacher's style by looking at their walls. They may be exuberant and busy or sparse and minimalist. Some rely heavily on laminated pre-made resources from the internet, while others create displays from scratch. Some tend towards a more neutral colour scheme in consideration of children with autistic spectrum disorder (ASD), in an attempt to avoid sensory overload and overstimulation. As Hanley et al. explain:

> A heavily decorated classroom may make children with ASD more susceptible to distraction from learning tasks than typically developing children.

In a study in which they tracked the eye movements of children with ASD, they found that:

> Not only did they look at the visually distracting background more than typically developing children in both story and lesson videos, but they looked more at the background than the teacher.[1]

What's universal, however, is that teachers and children like to adorn the walls with displays – in whichever visual format suits them – that play very different roles in the classroom. We think it's worth taking a moment here to consider why we put up displays. It can be time-consuming, so we want to know that our efforts have a purpose. Two purposes immediately spring to mind – to celebrate the children's work and to create tools for learning – but we'd like you to think deeper. If we know what we want our displays to do, and what impact we want them to have, then it becomes easier to design good-quality displays that will benefit the children in a myriad of different ways.

---

1    Mary Hanley, Mariam Khairat, Korey Taylor, Rachel Wilson, Rachel Cole-Fletcher and Deborah M. Riby, Classroom Displays – Attraction or Distraction? Evidence of Impact on Attention and Learning from Children with and without Autism, *Developmental Psychology*, 53(7) (2017): 1265–1275. Available at: http://dro.dur.ac.uk/20263/.

| Reasons | Celebration of children's work | Tools to aid learning |
|---|---|---|
| **Examples** | Mounted art work.<br><br>Finished prices of redrafted and edited writing.<br><br>Photos of science experiments accompanied by written-up reports about the hypotheses and methods.<br><br>Visual maths work, like shape nets, graphs, bar charts, etc.<br><br>Finished pieces of craft work, like puppets from DT, or printouts of computing projects. | Number lines.<br><br>Alphabet strips.<br><br>Punctuation prompts.<br><br>Synonyms for the four operations in maths.<br><br>Methods for working out how to approach two-step maths problems.<br><br>English and maths working walls featuring strategies, shared writing and worked examples.<br><br>Tricky words displays.<br><br>Phoneme family posters. |
| **Purposes** | To celebrate effort.<br><br>To celebrate achievement.<br><br>To show how the children have progressed.<br><br>To create an aesthetically pleasing display.<br><br>To show other classes in school what the class has been working on.<br><br>To share ideas and techniques with other classes in school. | To provide tools to help the children in their work.<br><br>To remind the children what the non-negotiables are in their work.<br><br>To help children with special educational needs (SEN).<br><br>As a resource for teachers to refer to during whole-class teaching.<br><br>To enable the children to access scaffolding and support without asking for help.<br><br>To embed topical or technical vocabulary so that the children get used to using the language. |

If we're looking closer at the purpose of displays, we can see some other reasons for their use, and we realise that growth mindset displays can be really valuable.

## Giving the topic gravitas

When you give wall space to something in your classroom, you are giving a message to the children that you care about that issue and that you consider it to be important. We all know that when we love a lesson and feel excited by it, the children 'catch' that excitement. Therefore, if we put effort into putting up a display about growth mindset, it shows the children – as well as the parents and anyone else passing through our room – that we care about it and mean what we say.

## Interest

Posters and interesting displays will encourage the children to explore and take on new ideas and information. Good-quality images and considered titbits of information can ignite interest in the children. For example, Julia's display features a photograph of the children wearing their 'brain hats' to do some deep thinking.

## Examples of growth mindset in action in your class

In Julia's class, she often has children piping up with things like, 'Sammi's showing a growth mindset there, Mrs Stead!' and praising each other when they show the desired characteristics of growth mindset. It's great to document these observations on a display. You don't even need to use photos; transient notes written straight onto the backing paper, or onto mini-whiteboards stuck to the wall, will give celebratory, real-life examples to the children of how growth mindset is having a positive impact on their learning. Here, we can see how one Year 3 pupil, Jaks, improved his observational drawing of a runner bean.

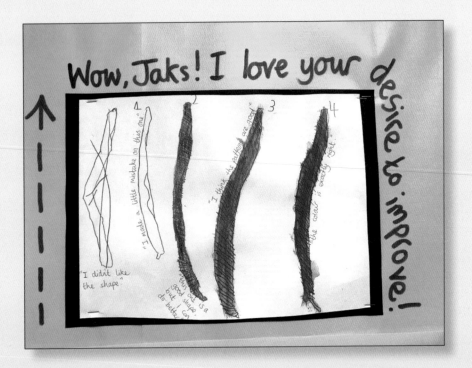

We began a 'to and fro' feedback process because he was determined to improve his picture, and he kept showing Julia and asking for advice. She encouraged him to try to see what he needed to do for himself and simply noted what he said. He drew the redrafts alongside each other, which made a lovely example of how he started to expect better of himself and strove to improve.

## Interactive encouraging displays

The more you make growth mindset fun, interactive and relevant to the children, the more they will embed it into their learning ethos. Consider creating interactive displays which are changed regularly. Julia has a 'Chance for a Challenge' board which changes every two weeks. The children can access it before they settle down for the register in the morning, or when they have a spare moment after finishing and checking their work. It's really popular, and she uses it as a tool to focus pupils' thoughts. If the children seem to need encouragement to think a little differently about a task, or need pushing to take a risk, she designs an interactive task that fits. For example, several boys were preoccupied with finding the 'correct' answer in a lesson on tessellation. It wasn't obvious what that was, and they didn't like the feeling of uncertainty. In the spirit of encouraging them to feel 'comfortable with feeling uncomfortable', Julia gave them the following task.

In this Chance for a Challenge activity, the pupils have a cardboard grid which needs filling with lots of different-shaped pieces that can, if set together in certain ways, tessellate. Some will go together, some won't. The aim is to cover the board with the pieces so that there are no gaps – similar to the retro game Tetris.

The variations in this task are – for all intents and purposes – limitless, and the pupils can work out a successful answer without the need to be 'correct' in a certain way. Julia thinks of it as growth mindset by stealth and skulduggery, as the children don't explicitly catch on to the agenda behind what she's doing – they just experience a fun challenge and reap the growth mindset rewards further down the line.

## SOME IDEAS TO MAGPIE

We dedicated a small area of a display to what we call 'Maths Eyes', a weekly 20-minute session in which we focus on high-level mastery questioning in maths. The whole class examines a photo – rich in maths content – which is displayed on the interactive whiteboard. Over the course of the week, children can add their ideas about the maths that they can 'see' to a physical copy which is posted on the wall. Julia asked a local optician for some spare lensless spectacle frames, which the children love putting on when they're looking for the maths contained in the image.

We also created a display to remind the children of the processes involved in their learning. This was a valuable lesson, and we wanted the children to constantly refer to the stages of learning during subsequent tasks. We began by looking at a series of statements that described stages in the learning process, but these were out of sequence and needed to be rearranged into a logical order. The resulting display acts as a visual reminder but, more importantly, because the pupils had discussed and ordered the flow of the learning stages, they had taken ownership of the process.

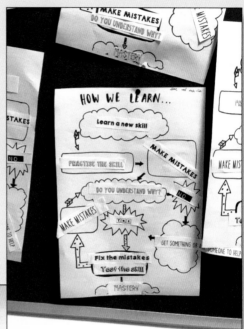

To further reinforce the value of the pupils taking ownership of their tools for learning, this was nicely presented alongside a reminder of the growth mindset strategies in the survival toolkit.

Another important display component is the seven features of growth mindset, to which we constantly refer and strive for in our classrooms. It's Julia's most-used tool for embedding growth mindset as it's so effective and easy to understand. We chose these seven features as we felt that they represented the most important areas of mindset, and they are the traits that we want to see weaving through all our pupils' work, interactions and learning behaviours. Once introduced, these become like classroom mantras, with children noting in their books the number of the trait they believe they have shown in that piece of work. Children congratulate each other when they notice each other 'being number 4', and they are always referring to the traits – embedding the goals and values which we hold dear. Furthermore, we've found that the presentation is important: it's amazing how much worth children attribute to something when it's in a frame! We've included in the list some examples of the sorts of things the children or teacher might say in relation to these points.

Children with a growth mindset:

1. Welcome a challenge. *'A challenge is good because if something was just easy all the time, we wouldn't learn anything from it. There's no point in doing something if we're not learning anything ...'*

2. Have a passion to learn. *'We get excited by new things and forging new connections in our brains. We come to school to build our knowledge and skills because it makes us into more intelligent human beings! It's exciting to develop and to see all the fascinating things there are all around us.'*

3. Believe you can work on your skills to get better. *'I might not be finding this easy, and I might not understand it fully, but with a bit more practice I can improve. Maybe I could think about this calculation in a different way – that might allow me to reach the answer. Mo Farah wasn't a champion the first time he went for a jog – it took work and effort to train to be the best.'*

4. Are inspired by the greatness in others. *'Amber is so good at remembering her French vocabulary. I might ask her if she has any tips. I really admire the way that other people avoid distractions during our daily mental maths practice. I'm going to try and be more like them. I love the pattern Amir has made with those blocks. I'm going to see if I can make one with the different plastic ladybirds.'*

5. Think mistakes are great because you learn from them. *'I want you to make mistakes, because then we can talk about them, and really understand the maths behind column multiplication. If we didn't make any mistakes, it would mean that I haven't guided you into anything new. Mistakes are how we dig deeper into everyone's understanding.'*

6. Keep going when things get tough. *'If I keep going, I'll have much more of a chance of understanding this work than if I just give up. If I quit now, the chance of me being successful is 0%. If I use all the tools I know to try to work this problem out, then I have every chance of being successful.'*

7. Know that hard work and effort are the keys to success. *'An accomplishment feels so much better if the task is tricky. It makes me feel like I've really improved and learnt something new that will help me in similar things. I know David is really good at playing the drums. He became good over time, though, because he worked hard on getting his rhythm just right. He wasn't a superstar overnight!'*

As we've mentioned, in Chapter 10 we'll go through lots of activities and lesson ideas that you can try out straight away with your own class. We've tested them all with our classes and often our pupils wanted to keep a record of their ideas, work and creations. From this we created a celebratory anthology of growth mindset work. We simply slipped pieces of work that best demonstrated this into a display folder. The children really enjoy looking back on their ideas during quiet reading time.

We also have a large Challenge Ocean display to act as a reminder of the analogy. It gives the children the vocabulary to use to help their reasoning and independence when they encounter challenge in their learning.

So far, we've given examples of how we have used displays to highlight the values and approaches to learning that we want to embed in the children's minds. However, we also allow displays to evolve out of the work that we are doing in class. In transition week at the start of Year 3, for example, we explored the children's beliefs about what makes a good learner and a good teacher. The discussions were really insightful, and it helped the children to realise that the only person who can take ownership and responsibility for your learning journey is you. You can find the full details of this activity in Chapter 10, in the lesson What's a Teacher? What's a Learner? Part 2. Of course, the ideas generated and the quality of the discussion would be different depending on the age of the children and the context of the school, not to mention the teacher delivering the activity, so be prepared to adapt the discussion in different directions. In this class, some of the children made a link with a tree – they observed that just as a tree grows over time, we grow as we learn. So we changed tack and wrote our ideas about what makes a learner and a teacher on paper leaves, to make a simple tree display. The visual metaphor supported the ideas we wanted to get across.

As another example, in nursery, we read *The Dot* by Peter H. Reynolds.[2] It's about a little girl who doesn't want to do the art work that her teacher is asking for. She assumes she's no good at painting, so simply splodges a dot on the paper. The next day, she finds that her dot has been framed by her teacher in celebration, and is slightly embarrassed that she is being praised despite not doing her best. She goes on to create a whole gallery of ever-better pieces of 'dot art', and eventually allows herself to enjoy her success. The story concludes with her helping another child to see past his 'I can't do that' attitude by setting him on a similar path.

---

2   Peter H. Reynolds, *The Dot* (London: Walker Books, 2004).

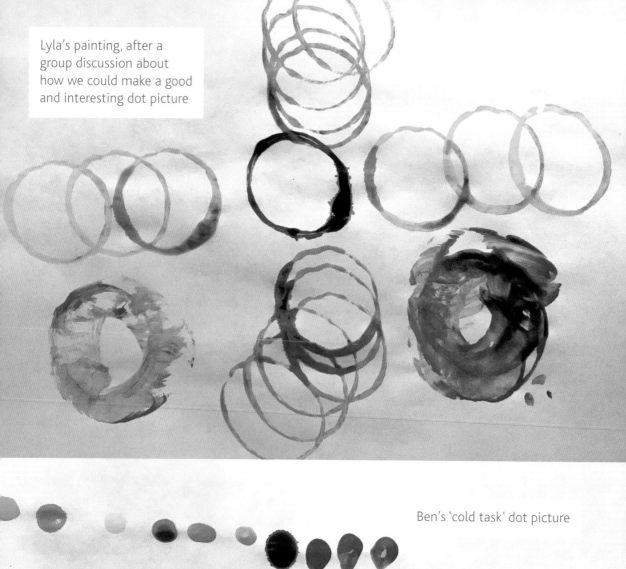
Lyla's painting, after a group discussion about how we could make a good and interesting dot picture

Ben's 'cold task' dot picture

After sharing the story with the children, we developed the idea of doing our very best work by putting in more effort. We did our first 'dot' with finger paint, and then decided how we could make them better. We looked at mandalas, and eventually created our finished pieces of art, inspired by the story. We have all seen work which is needlessly mediocre. Perhaps our expectations weren't high enough, or the children responded with work that didn't stretch their potential or ignite that precious feeling of achievement from having done their best. Reading *The Dot* is a great way of presenting this idea to the children – we can achieve far greater things if we work hard. Furthermore, the story format presents the message in a way that children can easily relate to. If you link the idea to work you've recently done in class, then the children will have a concrete reference point, and will be far better placed to understand the idea that hard work gets better results.

Julia decided to do a rudimentary experiment to test this idea out by comparing Lyla's and Ben's work. Lyla was four years and two months old at the time, and Ben was aged six years and three months. Both children were working at age-related expectations for creative areas of the curriculum. The main variable, other than age, was that Lyla had taken part in the nursery lesson in which the children had explored the story and been introduced to the concept of improving your work and developing the best version you can.

Notice how Lyla had included some symmetrical structures that she'd seen in the mandalas, and used regularity of colour. There is evidence of counting the dots, and she's experimented with moving the dot (the end of a cardboard tube dipped in paint) around.

Ben had simply been asked to draw an interesting, 'good' dot. He made a pattern and was pleased with himself for adding another dot each time he changed colour. What is striking is that there are few clues that the ages of the children are so wildly different. With some background teaching, Lyla's outcome was arguably more creative and careful than Ben's.

While this is probably the least scientific observation you'll find in a published book, it served its purpose of confirming what most teachers would instinctively claim: children have to know the purpose behind, and expectations of, their work, and want to do their best in order to produce work that befits their full potential. Granted, Lyla had looked at mandala designs and had seen work modelled, but this is a natural part of teaching. We model, teach and guide the children to find things out for themselves through carefully planned learning opportunities. Think of it like sharing learning objectives with children: if they know what they're aiming for, they'll have more chance of being successful. Ben was perfectly happy with his dots, but had he experienced the growth mindset aspect of the activity, he might have produced something far more advanced.

What fits in one classroom may not fit in another, but one point remains true: there needs to be a clear reason behind our displays. They take time and effort to construct, and they need to be more than just decoration. When a display serves more than one purpose, it starts to have more impact on the children and their learning. We don't want wallpaper; we want fuel for pupils' minds, virtual ladders for them to climb up to the next stage of their learning, and a reinforcement of the good they've already achieved.

## Chapter 5

# CHILDREN'S SELF-REGULATION AND AUTONOMY

Self-regulation is when learners want to do a task for its inherent value – not to please the teacher or because it's something they 'just have to do'. We absolutely need the children to get on board and become masters of the intended mindset. It sometimes feels like initiatives come and go in primary schools, but the change that we can see in children when they develop a growth mindset shows that it is a way of living that will see them into adulthood, rather than a passing fad. However, this can only happen if the children willingly join the teacher on the roller coaster of changing the way in which they see their learning.

Growth mindset is more of a sense of being than it is a skill, as the children become motivated by intrinsic drives. If these drives become second nature, and part of their natural learning behaviours, then their idea of learning as something that is given to them by the teacher is eroded, as is their reliance on the teacher. When Julia was in the early weeks of teacher training, she saw the children as empty vessels into which to pour knowledge and understanding. However, she quickly learnt that it's by enabling the children to see things for themselves that you really make a difference. If they want to learn because of their intrinsic drives, then they are far more likely to do so in a way that will have an impact. When working out what made classroom environments conducive to fostering intrinsic motivation, Carlton and Winsler concluded that:

> Children need structure that allows for free exploration. They should be challenged and allowed to set their own goals and to evaluate their own successes. Setting the environment up for this type of learning is of utmost importance. Activities need to be carefully selected to provide the correct amount of challenge and to engage curiosity. Guidance and scaffolding techniques properly utilized will help children develop to their highest potential.[1]

Children need to have control over their learning, but alongside careful scaffolding and support. We like to think of these drives as target practice. Children take aim at a

---

1   Martha P. Carlton and Adam Winsler, Fostering Intrinsic Motivation in Early Childhood Classrooms, *Early Childhood Education Journal*, 25(3) (1998): 159–166 at 165. DOI: 10.1023/A:1025601110383

target in their learning: a goal or end point. The more arrows they have to fire, the more likely they are to hit the target. These arrows could represent things like making sure they have opportunities to practise, the encouragement to have a go despite feeling uncomfortable, or being supported at home with their learning. A full complement of arrows (intrinsic drives) is a gold-plated set of tools which will help them to achieve a successful end result, even if not all of them are needed in every learning activity.

Having more intrinsic drives gives children a better chance of success. The goal for us as teachers is to support children in the journey towards embracing and living these intrinsic drives.

What drives a child with a growth mindset?

- The opportunity to experience a challenge.
- Excitement about learning something new.
- Wondering what other learners have to offer them.
- Accepting that something might not work.
- A desire to improve themselves.
- The opportunity to improve.
- Positivity without fear.

Even though we – as interested adult practitioners – can see the value of these kinds of drivers, our aim is to make the children in our class believe in them and adopt them as motivation in their daily lives. So how do we do this?

# METACOGNITION

The Education Endowment Foundation (EEF) explain that:

> Metacognition and self-regulation approaches aim to help pupils think about their own learning more explicitly, often by teaching them specific strategies for planning, monitoring and evaluating their learning.[2]

It's about understanding the process of learning so that pupils know where they are and how to achieve the knowledge that they are aiming for. They have to explore and think about the new knowledge before they can start to skilfully use and manipulate it.

The EEF go on to clarify that:

> Self-regulated learning can be broken into three essential components:

- cognition – the mental process involved in knowing, understanding, and learning;

- metacognition – often defined as 'learning to learn'; and

- motivation – willingness to engage our metacognitive and cognitive skills.

We find that one of the clearest ways to get children to take ownership of their learning is by questioning. Tofade, Elsner and Haines produced a great study about effective and non-effective questioning. Although the study took place in a higher education

---

2   See https://educationendowmentfoundation.org.uk/evidence-summaries/teaching-learning-toolkit/meta-cognition-and-self-regulation/.

setting, the findings are applicable to all educators. They conclude by recommending that teachers:

> formulate a wider range of questions that not only stimulate the recall of important factual, conceptual, and procedural knowledge but also requires learners to analyze, evaluate, and create.[3]

In order to help the pupils to structure their thoughts and actions, we like to question them before, during and after the learning process or task. Questioning beforehand guides the children regarding what will make the task successful; it helps them to see the value of their efforts and actions during the learning and gives them ideas about how to start. During the task, questioning draws the children into line with its aims and helps them to see the good in what they've already achieved and the possibilities that they haven't yet thought of. It also gives those children who are working well the opportunity to think more deeply and achieve an even more masterful outcome. Afterwards, children can reflect on their learning and see what went well and why. If they are thinking about the thought processes they went through, they are well placed to decide how they might respond differently next time to achieve even greater success. They can draw on each other's responses to questions and plan a way forward to use in future.

The best way for a child to improve their learning behaviour is for them to understand it and to become the protagonist in their own story. Nobody else should care about their learning as much as they do – and this will be especially true once they reach adulthood. That's the aim behind getting the children to care and to become autonomous. Can children identify what else they need to learn in order to achieve the objective? Where will they get this from? Do you need to model it? Are there success criteria they can use?

So, if we imagine the learning journey during a task as being in an aeroplane that we need to take off, fly and land, here are some ideas for questions to explore at the beginning (meta take-off), middle (meta flight) and end (meta landing) of learning:

---

3    Toyin Tofade, Jamie Elsner and Stuart T. Haines, Best Practice Strategies for Effective Use of Questions as a Teaching Tool, *American Journal of Pharmaceutical Education*, 77(7) (2013), Article 155. Available at: https://www.ncbi.nlm.nih.gov/pmc/articles/PMC3776909/.

## Take-off

Can you think of two different ways of approaching this task?

Can you think of a sentence that could start you off?

What might be the trickiest part of this task?

Can you think of any other work you've done that uses the same skills you'll be using today?

How could you split this work up so that it feels manageable?

## Flight

What is going well?

What is tricky? Can you think of something or someone to help?

What are you most proud of in this work so far?

Have you changed your plans? Why? Why not?

Have you noticed anyone else doing anything interesting that you could use in your own learning?

Can you think of one thing in your work so far that you could make even better?

## Landing

What new skills have you learnt today?

What would you do differently next time?

How could you use these new skills in other lessons or activities?

What resources will you choose to support you next time?

Would this work be good enough to be classed as your 'best effort'? Why? Why not?

What questions do you still have about the learning? If you don't have a question, think of a similar problem and solve it.

Questions like these make the implicit *explicit* for the children. We can't just assume or hope that they will think about their learning – we have to make it visible.

Take a look at the planning format, displayed on page 79, that Julia has used recently in maths with her Year 3 children. It's called the S plan and we were introduced to it by Jo Harbour, a maths mastery specialist, during Cambridge Maths Hub training.[4] It's revolutionised the way in which we see planning, and makes the planning visible and tangible for the pupils too.

You begin by writing your objective on the final sticky note at the bottom of the S and then think of all the tiny steps necessary to get to that end point. Each small step is on a sticky note, so that they can be switched around as necessary. Resources are noted on the right, and key questions and/or phrases can be listed on the left. It is a clear structure for the teacher to plan the learning journey around.

Another idea would be to create a map to help the children see the learning route clearly. You could even stylise it to look like a map if you have the inclination! The key idea is that the clearer the end point, and the more visible the learning journey, the more likely the children are to reach the destination. If you construct it as a class or in small groups, the children will feel ownership of it, adding to their autonomy in learning. If the children confidently know what they're doing, the whole journey becomes visible and supported. On page 80 you will find an alternative example of how you could share the learning journey on an interactive whiteboard. The older the pupils, the more detail you can share.

In Key Stage 1 and even in the early years foundation stage (EYFS), the journey can still be made visible – a good idea would be to use pictures or representations of each step instead of writing, and to only include three or possibly four steps. Making a journey visible applies to whatever skill you're teaching. Even a successful footballer has had to master the skills journey (see illustration on page 81).

---

4    Maths Hubs provide specialist training across the country. See http://www.mathshubs.org.uk/find-your-hub/cambridge-maths-hub/ for details.

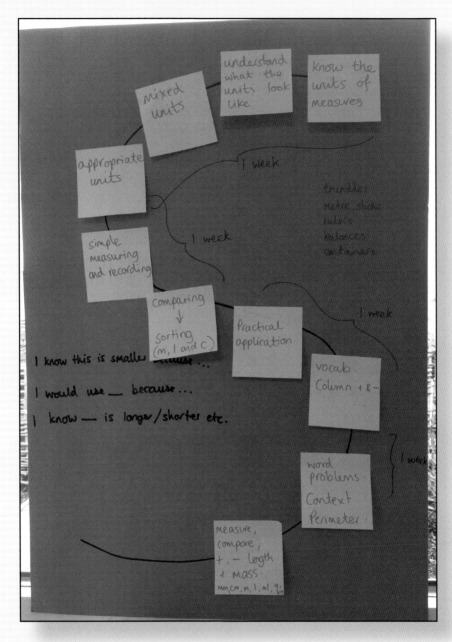

Mrs Stead's S plan for maths

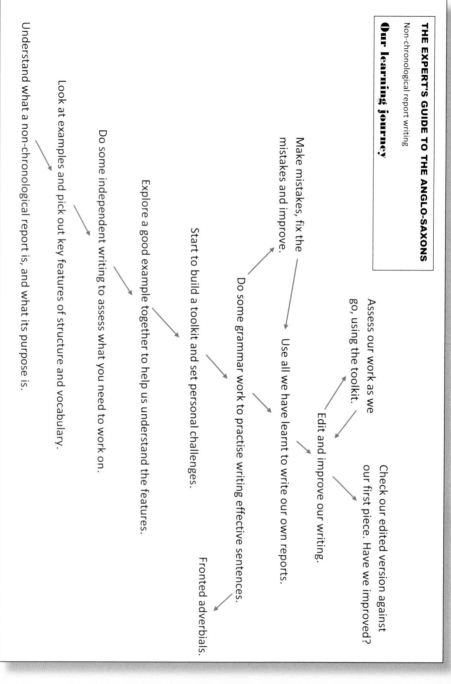

**THE EXPERT'S GUIDE TO THE ANGLO-SAXONS**

Non-chronological report writing

**Our learning journey**

Check our edited version against our first piece. Have we improved?

Assess our work as we go, using the toolkit.

Edit and improve our writing.

Make mistakes, fix the mistakes and improve.

Use all we have learnt to write our own reports.

Do some grammar work to practise writing effective sentences.

Start to build a toolkit and set personal challenges.

Fronted adverbials.

Explore a good example together to help us understand the features.

Do some independent writing to assess what you need to work on.

Look at examples and pick out key features of structure and vocabulary.

Understand what a non-chronological report is, and what its purpose is.

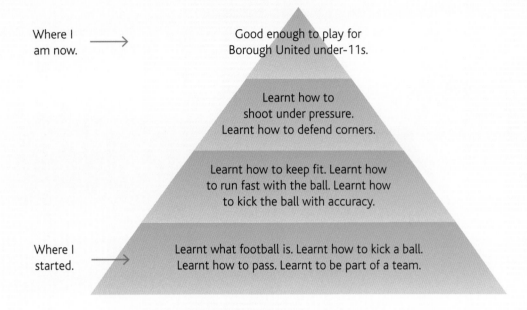

Where I am now. → Good enough to play for Borough United under-11s.

Learnt how to shoot under pressure. Learnt how to defend corners.

Learnt how to keep fit. Learnt how to run fast with the ball. Learnt how to kick the ball with accuracy.

Where I started. → Learnt what football is. Learnt how to kick a ball. Learnt how to pass. Learnt to be part of a team.

# BLOOM'S TAXONOMY - MAKING LEARNING VISIBLE FOR TEACHERS AND PUPILS

In 1956, Benjamin Bloom created his taxonomy of educational objectives. It was a way of clarifying these for both teachers and learners – allowing everyone to see what they were trying to achieve. This work positions Bloom as the forefather of the approaches that we have described so far in this chapter, and paved the way for our understanding of metacognition. Revised by Anderson and Krathwohl, it details a hierarchy of cognitive processes that learners go through in order to really understand something new.[5] These processes are conceptualised as a continuum along which we take a child, to guide them to a deeper and more embedded understanding. It's crucial that both teacher and learner share in this process, and that the reasons behind what we are doing are clear. The levels in the triangle on page 82 show the necessary foundations that must be built in a child's understanding before the next level can be achieved.

---

5    Lorin W. Anderson and David R. Krathwohl (eds), *A Taxonomy for Learning, Teaching, and Assessing: A Revision of Bloom's Taxonomy of Educational Objectives* (London: Pearson, 2000).

Have a think about a new topic in maths that you've recently taught – for Julia, this might be equivalent fractions. Trying to assign your teaching sequence to Bloom's levels is a thought-provoking activity. Did you leave any gaps, or omit a level altogether? It's when we use these as stepping stones on the learning journey that real embedded learning can take place.

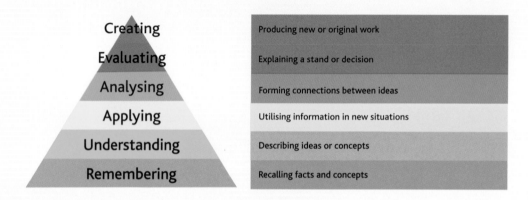

Bloom's taxonomy

Graphic adapted from Vanderbilt University Center for Teaching, Nashville, Tennessee

# CURIOSITY INSTEAD OF FEAR

In order for children to feel that mistakes are a positive part of learning, it is imperative that they feel their classroom is a safe place (as we explored in Chapter 3). When they feel safe and supported, the idea of getting things wrong isn't scary. The goal is to establish the classroom environment as a place where there is no such thing as a silly question, and where everything is an opportunity to grow and to learn. However, there's a difference between the security of pupils' comfort zones and the type of security we want to achieve. In an interview, one teacher summed this up precisely:

> "We'll purposefully try to put them in situations where they'll be uncomfortable, and yet not feel vulnerable – it's a kinda fine line we walk – and

then provide opportunities for them to work their way through it and find some success," Clark said.[6]

Done skilfully and regularly, these kinds of situations foster the soft skills of resilience and confidence in an *eventual* success that we often find so hard to teach. When pupils have been in this kind of situation, you can support them in deconstructing the task and working through it. Why was it challenging? What did we do to overcome the challenge? How did we feel at different points in the activity?

"It just reinforces the fact that understanding the first time you hear something isn't the goal," Clark said. "Smart isn't being right fast. It's working through things and understanding things eventually."

How can we support this process? We could:

- Set activities which deliberately involve trial and error. This happens all the time in maths and science and can lead to exciting discoveries.

- Set the pupils a problem and give them free rein to try out different solutions.

- Get the pupils to work in groups on one problem. One pupil records the trials and errors they experience.

- Celebrate and share plans and 'jottings' in maths lessons. Use them as a stimulus for discussing the importance of practice. Can the pupils spot any mistakes?

- Encourage pupils to embrace trial and error in their written work. For instance, by starting again, showing their working out or writing notes in the margin.

- Model trial and error in front of the whole class, talking them through it as you go. For example, 'So this mistake has been helpful for me because I learnt that ...'

This links nicely to rewards in the classroom. As we've already discovered, children should seek to learn for its intrinsic value, not to gain recognition, praise or reward from the teacher. What they achieve in the end is almost irrelevant, as we must change our approach to praise and reward *effort* rather than outcome. Almost daily in Julia's classroom, she says, 'It's good that it's tricky because if it was easy, there'd be no point in

---

6   Jim Clark, quoted in Katrina Schwartz, How to Weave Growth Mindset into School Culture, *Mind Shift* [blog] (2 October 2015). Available at: https://www.kqed.org/mindshift/42159/how-to-weave-growth-mindset-into-school-culture.

doing it – you wouldn't be learning anything!' Another common refrain is, 'Wow, you've found a much easier way of showing your working out on that question – well done!' Effort is the positive behaviour that deserves recognition.

This is a tricky point, as we don't want the pupils to *then* become motivated by gaining praise for their efforts. We therefore need to teach them explicitly about praise and effort, and explain that they won't always get that praise, so they shouldn't become reliant on it. The ethic of putting effort in will bring its own rewards throughout their learning lives. Hard work is the key to success, and by praising effort we are prais-ing what leads to success. Sure, we could praise a correct answer. However, praising effort is going to help that child when, instead of practising calculations in nursery, she is revising for her medical degree finals. Or perhaps when she's trying to bounce a basketball into a net when she's 50 years old. We don't want the medical student to expect to receive a pat on the head for getting the answers correct – we want her to be motivated to put in the effort before sitting the exam. Praising what matters draws children into beneficial habits – the habits of self-regulation, intrinsic motivation and a willingness to work hard because the reward is embedded in the act of doing your best.

Consider the following scenario, which is likely to be seen playing out in classrooms across the country every day. A Year 1 English lesson is going on, and the children have been asked to add capital letters in the correct places in three separate sentences. Elodie works through the task independently in about five minutes and gets everything correct. She worked conscientiously and didn't particularly rush, but she found the task easy enough that it wasn't a major challenge. Her teacher was thrilled that her answers were correct and gave her a house point for her 'hard work'. Elodie's happy, the teacher feels like she's done a good job, so all is well. Or is it?

What has Elodie learnt from the reward of the house point?

My teacher loves it when I get the answers right.

I'm clever at capital letters because I did them all right the first time.

If I'd made a mistake, I probably wouldn't have got a house point.

84

Jim isn't as good at English as I am because he took longer and didn't get a house point.

Doing it quite quickly was a good thing.

I hope I get it all right next time - then I'll get another house point.

Is that what we want to foster? There is little autonomy or self-motivation in the lessons Elodie has taken from that house point. If, however, the teacher had shown excitement about Elodie's effort, and employed some good questioning techniques to further her understanding, Elodie would have learnt something different:

My teacher realised that I'd worked hard.

I loved it when she asked me something a bit trickier - I was proud of myself.

I'm good at trying my best to be accurate.

My favourite part of that task was when I had to explain to Jim about how to use capital letters in people's names.

Next time, maybe I'll add some of my own examples underneath.

It's a habit to get into, but when you routinely praise effort, determination and trying again, you are teaching the children to value these traits in themselves. In time, this becomes the norm, and the pupils understand that we're looking for these traits over an 'easy win' end result. An easy outcome is just not worthwhile compared with when we have to think and persevere at a task. As the producer John Lloyd says:

> I do have at home the most ridiculous number of awards for what I have done, which is nice in terms of being patted on the back, yet it does cure you of caring about what other people say about you. Ultimately you must have your own standard of what is good enough. The real rewards are intrinsic, not extrinsic, and the pleasure of doing something well is of itself interesting and rewarding.[7]

In Chapter 12 we'll look at this more in relation to rewards from parents and schools.

## ROLE MODEL, ROLE MODEL, ROLE MODEL

The trick to embedding growth mindset values in your classroom is role modelling and being a real-life example of a person embodying growth mindset. Not just any person, either, but likely the most important adult outside of their home environment. This is our modus operandi as teachers – we role model in our interactions in class every day. We show children the way. We make mistakes every day, and can use these mistakes to show our own resilience, determination and positivity in the face of challenge.

We've probably all made a spelling error in front of our pupils. How we respond shows whether we're being a growth mindset role model or not. Valuing mistakes yourself will show the children that there is no fear to be found in learning situations.

---

7   John Lloyd, quoted in Nicholas Wroe, Laughing Matters, *The Guardian* (11 April 2009). Available at: https://www.theguardian.com/culture/2009/apr/11/interview-john-lloyd-comedy-producer.

Personal, social, health and economic (PSHE) education should guide your whole school in how to treat others, coupled with the values embedded in assemblies and your own manner with the children. The way in which you treat people should be inextricably linked with your growth mindset ideals. An environment in which children support each other, and everyone's needs are nurtured, has to become the norm. We can't accept a culture of ridicule or undermining others. We know how to role model. We have to be watchful of our actions and language, to demonstrate all the things that we know encourage a growth mindset. That applies to the language we use about ourselves just as much as to how we speak to the children. Our external voice in the classroom will become the children's inner voice. They'll talk to themselves internally during their learning – using the words, tone and ideas that they hear from us during the school day. It's a logical sequence of events. We expect something of our pupils: we model it: the pupils use that modelling: they reach the higher expectations we held. It's a bit like the Pygmalion effect:

> when we expect certain behaviors of others, we are likely to act in ways that make the expected behavior more likely to occur.[8]

When we've got our pupils talking in a way which is conducive to learning and self-improvement, then they're set for their learning lives – and for positivity in other areas of their lives too.

---

8   Robert Rosenthal and Elisha Y. Babad, Pygmalion in the Gymnasium, *Educational Leadership*, 43(1) (1985): 36–39 at 36.

# Chapter 6
# HIGHER-ORDER THINKING

We'd like you to imagine giving your class a piece of paper with a triangle drawn on it. You then instruct them to, 'Complete this picture in the right way.'

Your class might have a few immediate thoughts:

- There is a correct way – what if I don't know what it is?

- I don't understand – I must have missed the point.

- I'm worried that I should know the right answer – should I copy my friend?

- Should I ask what my teacher means?

- What pens am I meant to be using?

- Should I use colour?

The list could go on. With the implication of the words 'right way', the teacher is putting a heavy and burdensome limit on the task. It instils worry and fixed mindset thoughts in the learners. Children feel 'boxed' into the task. Phrased in a different way, there could have been limitless possibilities for the children to express their ideas.

Instead of the first instruction, imagine you'd said, 'Complete this picture in your own way.'

Julia imagined this, and then tested it out on her Year 3 class. On page 90 you will see, first, what they produced when they were concerned with the 'right way', and, immediately below, the vastly different results when they were afforded greater freedom.

The boundaries and limits had gone. The children each drew a different picture, rather than generating similarly non-descript outcomes. They used different types of pencils and pens, chose colours, expressed their personalities, spent far more time and care over their picture than in the first task and actually *created* something. The removal of the word 'right' totally changed the outcome.

Granted, our activities in school are likely to be far more robust and learning-orientated, but the idea remains as strong: putting limits on our pupils through the language we use – even if we don't mean to or realise that we are – sets the ceiling low and stifles

| Concerned with the 'right way' | | |
| --- | --- | --- |
| Amy | Kyle | Masie |
|  |  | 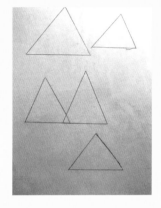 |
| | Especially noteworthy here is the obvious anxiety of 'getting it right', shown by the numerous crossings out, and the arrow in the top right corner directing Julia to the one he intended as the final iteration. | |

| Given greater freedom | | |
| --- | --- | --- |
| Amy | Kyle | Masie |
|  |  |  |

creativity. Marks undertook a case study which revealed that the notion of fixed ability is still widely held by teachers in England:

> Teachers and pupils still act as if individuals come hard-wired with a fixed-ability, adjusting – and often limiting – experiences and expectations accordingly.[1]

She goes on to explain what we could have if we disassociate ourselves from the idea that children are 'in the blue group for maths' because they'll never get it:

> in the absence of fixed-ability thinking it should be possible to provide all pupils with access to an engaging and rewarding mathematics curriculum rather than, as we currently have, one which only allows selected pupils to succeed.[2]

So what does this mean for us in the classroom? If a teacher's bread and butter is questioning, how can we ask questions to further the children's understanding? We've seen how questioning can be the making or breaking of a task, so let's explore how we can use effective questioning in our growth-mindset classroom to take full advantage of every interaction and activity.

It's worth considering why we question at all. In our classrooms we see three main reasons:

1. To assess understanding.

2. To encourage learners to listen to, consider and act upon one another's responses.

3. To further and structure a learner's thoughts by paving the way for them to think about the next idea or answer for themselves.

We can see the growth-mindset thread weaving through all three reasons, not least in number 2 – in which we want the children to act as support and scaffolding for each other. Our questioning has to facilitate children taking charge of their own learning. The most effective questioning can achieve all three of these aspirations, but that

---

1    Rachel Marks, 'The Blue Table Means You Don't Have a Clue': The Persistence of Fixed-Ability Thinking and Practices in Primary Mathematics in English Schools, *Forum*, 55(1) (2013): 31–44 at 36. Available at: http://doi.org/10.2304/forum.2013.55.1.31.
2    Marks, 'The Blue Table Means You Don't Have a Clue', 43.

involves crafting your questions with them in mind. When we only address one, our questioning isn't as valuable. In modern teaching, as we aim to limit teacher-talk, the time we spend on questioning needs to be gold standard – we need to make the most of every question. Morrison McGill says from his experience:

'teacher-talk' can (not solely) be a root-cause of poor behaviour and debilitate student's acquisition of knowledge and skill during a lesson. More often than not, I've observed many, many lessons and have watched teachers talk and talk.[3]

The more talking a teacher does, the less time is left for the children to investigate, reason, analyse and unpick the learning. If your questions represent good value – by comparing the time spent on them to how much progress they achieve – then the potential for learning, and the children's true mastery of skills, is far superior.

# ASSESSING UNDERSTANDING

At the bottom of the questioning effectiveness scale is finding out if a pupil can respond correctly about something you have just said, presented or taught. It's the equivalent of ticking a learning objective or not. It's functional, but it could be so much more productive. At the other end of the scale, we have questions that feel more like a window into the pupil's brain. We can craft a question that allows us not only to assess against an objective but to see just how far the pupil can take the learning. Our assessment can break past what we *need* to know, and really show us the potential of the child's thinking. We want the question to show us the limit of the child's understanding – and that might be far higher than we expect. It works the same way as grouping children by ability. If we limit them to an ability band, we limit what they are exposed to, and what they could show us. It's the Pygmalion effect that we noticed earlier, presenting itself in the inverse form of limiting our pupils by our own limiting behaviours and expectations. We need to give them the chance to surprise us.

---

3   Ross Morrison McGill, #TeacherTalk, *Teacher Toolkit* [blog] (n.d.). Available at: https://www. teachertoolkit.co.uk/teachertalk/.

effectiveness

Can the child show you – over the course of their answer – that they have made a link, realised something about the content for themselves or broken through the ceiling of what has been presented to them, to show secure, developed understanding?

Can the child explain the knowledge to their peers in a way that makes sense?

Can the child explain why they believe their answer is correct?

Can the child apply their knowledge to something related to what you've just taught?

Has the child retained key facts about what you have just taught?

Can the child correctly answer a question about what you have just taught?

Questioning for assessment: scale of effectiveness

effectiveness

Is there another way to work out what a quarter of 4 is, not following the way I've shown you today?

Is it always true that you can divide a number by 4 to find a quarter? How can you be sure?

James said that he thought the answer was 4. Where do you think he went wrong?

How do you know that a quarter of 12 is 3? Give me proof.

If we know a quarter of 12 is 3, what would a quarter of 120 be?

How can you work out what a quarter of 12 is? Show me.

What is a quarter of 12?

Scale of effectiveness: examples

# ENCOURAGING OTHERS TO RESPOND AND GROW

In a class of engaged learners, it's really effective to use your questioning as a covert way of challenging the whole class' thinking. They don't realise it, but as your questioning techniques become more honed and mature, engaging with the questions becomes irresistible, whether a verbal answer is requested or not. Engaging questions help build relationships between pupils and teachers, giving the chance for articulate and meaningful conversations to develop. This is infectious! Children are naturally drawn to conversations that challenge them to understand something new. One of Julia's favourite off-plan moments was when a Year 4 class became enthralled by the concept of income tax and VAT, because it was new and required careful thought. True story – we promise! This engagement means that children are increasingly motivated to learn. They become inspired by others and see what they could achieve themselves. The exposure to others' answers and ideas is a springboard for them to have deeper thoughts.

As children build their metacognitive verbal fluency, they can use it in discussions with each other. When they can ask each other questions that engage and deepen learning, think how much more valuable and meaningful these common classroom practices become:

- Paired talk – children discuss their ideas and respond to what the teacher has just said or asked. It's a great way to limit teacher-talk and keep them on task during whole-class teaching. It also means that no one can 'opt out' of the learning, as they are regularly engaging with the content and sharing their input.

- Peer-scaffolding – children can support and encourage each other, and share advice and suggestions. This can help when there is a perceived discrepancy in ability, or when a child could do with an injection of confidence.

- Peer-assessment – when children discuss their work together, they will have the skills to really pull it apart. With metacognitive skills, they can make meaningful comments and suggestions rather than the classic, 'You've done well. You've been neat.'

The fluency of *speech* is developed in the speaker, and the fluency of *thought* is developed in the listener. The more children get used to explaining their thoughts and being challenged to think about things in different ways, the more they become willing to interact in the conversations. It might start out as a scary type of communication, as there are no short answers to these kinds of questions. However, when this kind of questioning becomes the classroom norm, children become comfortable with questions as the vehicle to higher thoughts, complicated ideas and growing minds.

When Julia challenged her Year 2 class to think mathematically about a picture of lots of cats that she displayed on the whiteboard, she asked them what they could see. How many different ways could they find to explain the maths in the picture? Their responses are written on the slide below, in pacy lesson-note form. When there are no limits, there are no wrong answers, and children volunteer to say so much more.

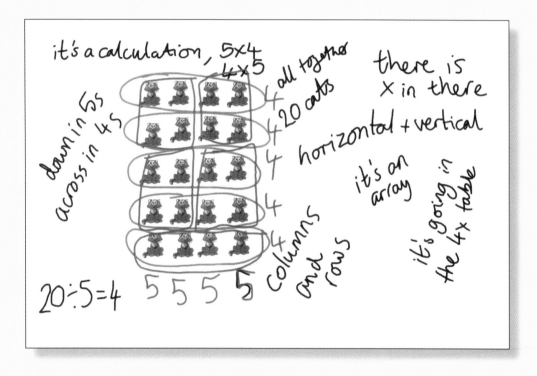

# PAVING THE WAY FOR THE NEXT, OR DEEPER, LEARNING POINT

So, we need some general question types that we can put into our teaching straight away. These questions should:

- Be open-ended.

- Require thought to answer.

- Encourage the pupil to be self-reflective in their answer.

- Pose more learning opportunities.

- Present opportunities for other pupils to listen and build on their own thoughts and learning.

- Encourage pupils to make links in their knowledge.

- Challenge pupils' thinking so they become more in tune with their logic.

Julia has the following questions displayed above the whiteboard, mostly so they're quick to access, and so we're consistent with the phrasing. The children can see and use them too, which backs up our supportive questioning ethos.

Are you sure?

How do you know?

What do you notice?

What's the same and what's different?

Can you convince me that ...?

Is there another way?

Can you imagine ...?

Do you mean ...?

In our experience, asking children 'Are you sure?' encourages them to self-check rather than rely on the teacher to validate their answer immediately – thereby cancelling out some of the thinking processes behind the learning. It takes them to the next level of thinking. They have to justify it for themselves before responding with a definite thought. It also works well if you ask this question when they've got something correct. They really have to know that they're right and, crucially, why.

Asking 'How do you know?' helps pupils become more reliant on themselves, and on each other's ideas and reasoning. 'What do you notice?' and 'What's the same and what's different?' get the children looking for patterns and links in their learning. These types of questions help children to develop the skill of generalising. They give you a peek into where the child's skill level is at that moment, and reveal how you can nudge them up to the next rung of their learning ladder, or clarify something to deepen their understanding.

Asking children 'Is there another way?' shows free-thinkers that they aren't wrong, and reinforces for the class that different methods can lead to the same conclusions. Asking children to *imagine* is a brilliant way of encouraging them to rely on their own creativity. The burden of thought is on them, rather than you. Using the final question – 'Do you mean ...?' – is questioning's version of insurance. It can really help a child to clarify their thinking if they aren't quite articulating it, or haven't learnt the necessary vocabulary to express their understanding. Use it sparingly, though, otherwise the benefit of the first two questions is reduced.

# QUESTIONING FOR GROWTH

Google saw the value of creativity and open-ended endeavour. They famously allow their employees something called 20% time, in which they are allowed to work on a 'pet project' for 20% of their working hours. They could work on an idea that interests them, challenges them or motivates them to create something. There is no stipulated direction. It works – the employees take the chance to follow their own instincts and question themselves. This activity resulted in serious successes for Google, including the development of Google News, Gmail and AdSense. The company's founders are quoted as saying:

> We encourage our employees, in addition to their regular projects, to spend 20% of their time working on what they think will most benefit Google [...]

This empowers them to be more creative and innovative. Many of our significant advances have happened in this manner.[4]

Wouldn't it be great to encourage this way of working in primary schools? We could give children time to work on their higher-order thinking skills and undertake highly creative and thought-provoking activities. We could explore questions like 'How could you combine a bus with a pencil?' Try it with your class – here are a couple of Julia's favourites from hers:

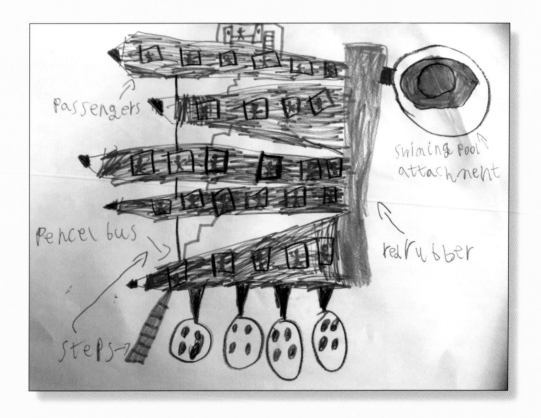

---

4    Larry Page and Sergey Brin, quoted in Jillian D'Onfro, The Truth About Google's Famous '20% Time' Policy, *Business Insider* (17 April 2015). Available at: https://www.businessinsider.com/ google-20-percent-time-policy-2015-4?r=US&IR=T.

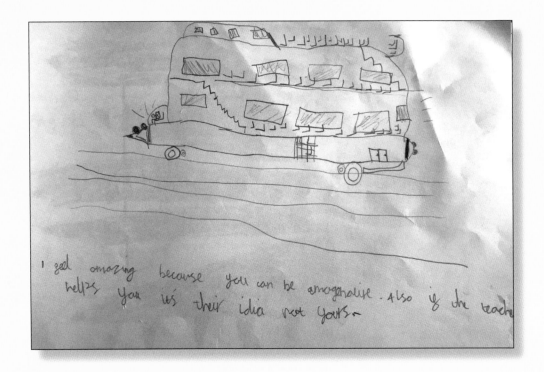

The talk about how a pencil would draw a line as the bus travelled around town was super. This time could be about nurturing problem-solving, creative or higher-order thinking skills – or about getting children ready for the demands of working life that await. Imagine the effect on a child of that time devoted to higher-level thinking: confidence in their own ideas, a willingness to experiment, a way of working that allows trial and error, a pace of working things out that can allow for deep experimentation ... the benefits of growth-mindset-conducive practice go on and on. It could include all children in the spirit of learning without limits – there are no exclusive rights on higher-order thinking. Perhaps gaps in attainment would close a lot quicker if all children were expected to think with these higher-order skills. Sparing just 30 minutes on a Friday afternoon could allow a small seed to be planted. 'Pet Project' time? The name could catch on!

Julia once tried the 'combine a bus with a pencil' task on colleagues in a staff meeting. It didn't go well. There was uncomfortable background chatter as they murmured, 'What are we meant to be doing?', 'I don't get what it means!' and 'I've no idea!' Her colleagues were not comfortable with what they perceived to be a strange idea and an unknown entity of a task. They were confused. Julia learnt a lot about how her colleagues approached the unknown, and by the end of the meeting they learnt that they had begun with a remarkably fixed mindset. Having seen the adults' reactions, Julia wanted to know more about how the children had felt when asked to do something strange and unknown, with hardly any guidance. Here are their responses verbatim:

Happy because you can do it by yourself.

I felt amazing because I could work it out myself. Then I am learning more if I do it.

It's helping me because when you go to work you have to work alone.

It's hard. But I'll try and when I get there, I'll be very proud of myself.

I feel stressed out because I need help with complicated stuff.

I sort of feel happy and sad – at the first bit I thought it would be too tricky, but in the end it was fun.

I feel calm because I don't have to explain stuff to my friends and I can just get on with my work.

I felt amazed because you can be imaginative. You can be colourful. If the teacher explains it to you, it makes it not as imaginative because it's their idea not yours.

What was heartening in terms of the children's developing mindset was that 20 out of the 25 in the class were glad that they'd had to approach the uncomfortable and unknown task with no help. Only five wished they'd had some help and guidance. So why do we want our learners to feel uncomfortable?

Blau reasoned that:

the major difference between less skilled and more productive learners is not their intelligence, but their willingness to endure disorientation, that feeling of being lost or confused. Confusion often represents an advanced state of understanding because the student who is confused is frequently the one who understands enough to see a problem.[5]

---

5    Sheridan D. Blau, *The Literature Workshop: Teaching Texts and Their Readers* (Portsmouth, NH: Heinemann, 2003), p. 21.

If we want children to welcome the confusion, we need to provide learning experiences that create that feeling in a *safe and productive* way.

> Since failure is not only part of life but also an essential part of the creative process, perhaps through carefully crafted learning experiences we can discover the "pleasures of difficulty".[6]

In children whose mindset is fixed, there is an unwillingness to welcome confusion. Newkirk argues that the reason lies in:

> the fear of embarrassment – that doing badly is less risky than admitting inadequacy by asking for help.[7]

Our task as teachers is to show children that asking for help – and accepting confusion and working through it – will result in the reward of success. The journey then feels good and the children learn the lifelong lesson that success is not a straight line – it involves discomfort, steps backward and acknowledging that things can be hard.

> Growth mindset gives one an ability to work though the initial discomfort of situations that don't make sense. Intelligence is not a matter of being smart – it is the capacity to view difficulty as an opportunity to stop, reassess, and employ strategies for making sense of problems.[8]

Let's think of some questions to help children be more comfortable with thinking in a different way. If we get them to answer questions that feel a little strange or unknown, then we create the right conditions for growth mindset. It teaches the children that it's okay if they face something that they haven't seen before or need time to think. They learn that the thinking energy is worth it – the effort is rewarded with great ideas.

---

6    Thomas Newkirk, *The Art of Slow Reading: Six Time-Honored Practices for Engagement* (Portsmouth, NH: Heinemann, 2012), p. 118.
7    Newkirk, *The Art of Slow Reading*, p. 135.
8    Newkirk, *The Art of Slow Reading*, p. 122.

What else could this be?

Think of as many different uses for this object as you can:

What would happen if:

1.   your tap stopped working?

2.   your head became rectangular overnight?

3.   the grass on the school field turned into spikes of hard plastic?

What could this be for?

What is this word?

Draw it. Use it in a sentence. Discuss it.

# PURE GROWTH MINDSET THINKING SKILLS

We've talked about getting the conditions right for children to develop higher-order thinking skills, and we've got them used to answering questions that make them feel a little uncomfortable or on the brink of the unknown. Sometimes, we need to make the signposts towards pure growth mindset thoughts more explicit, especially when we're introducing the growth mindset way of life into the classroom and getting the children to live and breathe it. This is nitty-gritty, espresso-strength growth mindset. It channels the children to really change the way they think, and justify everything they do within the ideals of growth, challenge and self-improvement.

As a teacher, what do you want when you are teaching children, whether it's the littlest 3-year-olds, or the big fish/little pond 11-year-olds? If we care about the child's learning journey, we would propose striving to encourage all our pupils to:

- Do their best.

- Challenge themselves.

- Not give up.

- Help others.

- Seek advice.

- Believe in their ability to succeed.

- Be resilient if things don't work out.

- Try to improve on their work as time goes on.

- Seek satisfaction from learning something new.

- Place value in the process of learning.

Even though we have these ideas in our well-toned teaching brains, the children sometimes need bringing round to this way of thinking. It's not always obvious to them how to live a growth mindset. Therein lies the crux of this book – we neead to support children to develop this, so they eventually have a nurtured, well-taught and well-developed growth mindset that has been nurtured and modelled for them. Questions can act as reminders of what we want to see from the children. Just a simple question can do so much:

· Remind.

· Make obvious.

· Lead thoughts.

· Make others in the class think.

· Clarify.

· Reinforce the importance of the idea.

The following questions are pure and strong like a shot of espresso – there is no way to escape the growth-mindset encouragement in these:

You're stuck?
Okay, what could
you use to
help you?

That mistake is
great because you
can learn from it.
What might you
learn?

What happened
today that made
you have to think
hard?

Where did it go wrong?
Can you think of a
way to make it
go right?

What did you
try hard at
today?

Keep going! What's
your next step?

What are you
going to do to
challenge yourself
today?

How could you
improve this
work?

What different
strategy could
you try?

Is this your best
work? How could
you make it your
best?

How will you
feel when
you 'get it'?

Is there someone
who has managed this
who could help you to
understand?

## Chapter 7

# THE ABILITY MYTH

Imagine that you have been asked to observe a group of students at an adult education centre. They all come from different walks of life and are learning to paint. The cohort have been together for a few months now and routines are established. When you walk around the work space you notice that some are using oil paints on large canvases, others are using watercolours or acrylics, but near the front are a small group who are using crayons and paper. You decide to go over and talk to this group. Their responses are revealing but unhelpful:

'We're not very good at painting, we need to master crayons first.'

'We're still practising how to draw basic objects. When we get better, we can try a more challenging still life.'

'I'm a red artist which means that I'm in the middle with my skill base. I go for artistic challenges that are not too easy but not too hard either. I wouldn't want to get stuck or make a mess of my canvas and have to start again because I did it wrong.'

Dissatisfied with what you have heard, and shocked by the group's self-judgements, you find the workshop leader for more information. You ask about how the group is set up and about how the sessions take the individual artist's existing skills into account.

'We do drawing and painting assessments at the beginning of each specific workshop and we find that some of our students haven't grasped the basics of pencil drawing. There's no point starting them off with paints if they can't do the fundamentals.'

'When we set out the focus for each workshop, we make sure there is something that everyone can access. We wouldn't want our students to struggle with something they just can't do. We're an inclusive group.'

'Sometimes we might split the focus into different parts, so all students must make marks with a drawing tool, some should add paint and a few could add details using another technique. Usually, we take the better artists and show them how they can add the details so that they can improve their work. We like to push the more-talented students.'

'Some of the participants come from homes where art was never a focus or deemed important. When the artists don't have support or encouragement around them, it's harder to motivate them and sometimes they are disengaged.'

'We've been working on brush strokes for months and some of our artists still can't hold the paintbrush properly. They're just not going to get there without lots of support.'

'We have been trying to encourage the artists to choose their own subject matter so that they can really take ownership of their work. We construct three options and label them brown, red and cerulean blue; the artists are able to choose which one they want to draw. We tend to find that the less-able artists always go for the brown still life, but it's important to involve them in the process.'

You have some questions:

- What is the group's perception of themselves as artists?

- When will the workshop leader provide the right learning tasks so that all the artists develop a new skill together?

- How will the students ever learn how to use the oil paints if they are not given the opportunity?

- Why are they enrolled in the class if they are not able to progress, as surely that's the point of taking part?

- Who on earth labelled the activities brown, red and cerulean blue?

- Have the painters mastered the crayons?

- Is it acceptable to box them up according to prior judgements of their ability?

- Does the workshop leader truly understand what the artists are capable of? Where is the evidence of this?

- Where are the opportunities for developing skills in other areas of art? Pottery, sculpture, abstract, contemporary, art history, chalks ... the list goes on!

Now, we know what you're thinking, 'Clearly they've used an exaggerated scenario to illustrate the pitfalls of ability grouping. I can see right through it.' We don't doubt it; you're clearly an insightful reader if you've bought this book. But just think about it for a minute: substitute the artists for pupils and painting for learning objectives and is it really a million miles off what takes place in hundreds, if not thousands, of classrooms?

How often do we talk about children using labels like low-ability, less-able, developing, emerging, triangles, squirrels, ladybirds and 'one-chillis'? (In this ranking system, one chilli is the least challenging and aimed at pupils who might be labelled as lower-ability, three chillies is the most challenging and designed for those labelled higher-ability or gifted and talented.) More worryingly, how *easy* is it to do this? We've tried really hard to change our vocabulary from low/high ability to low/high attaining and yet it is difficult to do this consistently when the majority of colleagues, systems and resources still refer to learners by their ability alone. In three of the schools we've worked in, that chilli challenge system of differentiation was well-versed. Children self-assess and choose which activity – which level of challenge – they feel suits them and their learning at that time. Done well, it can enable pupils to better access the content. But done in the context of ability grouping, it creates the fear. Words matter. Labels limit. Children *know*. Ask yourself this: if we are trying to cultivate growth mindset in our impressionable pupils, if we are working hard to challenge the limitations they put on themselves when they say they can't do something and if we are trying to encourage them to see that their potential is boundless, then why on earth do we imply such low expectations? More importantly, how can we change the way in which we approach differentiation in the average lesson in order to reflect this shift in ideology around fixed ability? In a safe classroom the agenda must go from ability to *capability*.

A few years ago, while Ruchi was teaching a Year 4 class, a colleague came to see her during break time. She had a sorry look on her face. When Ruchi pressed her, she revealed that she had been trying to explain a fairly difficult concept to Holly, but that Holly had been confused throughout. Holly usually needed more practice than her peers, her resilience was generally low and she had learnt to put little effort into her work as she was used to an adult coming over to help her.[1] Ruchi's colleague explained that it was clear that Holly wasn't quite getting it. She kept trying but her face must've shown her weariness. Eventually, Holly raised her eyebrows and said, 'The trouble is, Miss, you're talking to a mild.'

Aged eight, Holly had already developed a deterministic and fixed view of her own capacity to succeed. Despite good intentions, she had inadvertently been labelled as 'mild' – the 'spicy' tasks were reserved for the clever kids, something Holly wouldn't dare to attempt for fear of failure. What had started out as a progressive approach to differentiation had been watered down into a low-ability, medium-ability, high-ability hierarchy. Rather than empowering pupils to choose the activity that best suited them in terms of challenge, they had been capped by their perceived ability and, in turn, had very fixed ideas about their own capability. On a superficial level, children were given the autonomy to 'choose' their learning task, but this resulted in inadvertent ability groups. In no uncertain terms, this approach was failing our pupils, widening gaps and having a negative impact on mindset growth. As a result, outcomes were increasingly difficult to improve.

Now, we're not knocking a three-step approach *per se*. What's more important is what informs these learning tasks: that all pupils are allowed opportunities to aim high, that they can work with a range of peers, that they can self-assess and discuss how their learning is going and that they know and understand the processes involved.

Let's look at two teachers who are each planning a grammar objective in writing.

| Teacher A | Teacher B |
| --- | --- |
| Knows their pupils well and uses writing assessment data to track progress. When designing a lesson | Knows their pupils well and wants to assess how well they understand different sentence types before |

---

1   This is another example of learned helplessness. In one study, Dweck and Diener explored some of the reasons why helpless children (those reliant on adult intervention or support) show a decrease in performance following failure, compared to their mastery-orientated counterparts who often show enhanced performance under the same conditions. See, Carol I. Diener and Carol S. Dweck, An Analysis of Learned Helplessness: Continuous Changes in Performance, Strategy, and Achievement Cognitions Following Failure, *Journal of Personality and Social Psychology*, 36(5) (1978): 451–462.

around simple, compound and complex sentences, they know that some pupils are still struggling to write compound sentences and will find complex sentences tricky to identify. The teacher decides to do some whole-class teaching around simple and compound sentences and split the independent task into two: identifying and writing simple sentences *or* identifying and writing compound sentences. The teacher or TA will work with the group who need the most support. The extension task will move children on to identifying and writing complex sentences as a precursor to the following day, when the whole class will move on and look at this together.

designing their next lesson. They decide to start with an open-ended activity to determine the children's starting points. Through this, they realise that while most children can write simple and compound sentences, they are unable to define, identify or explain the difference. They are also unable to explain how the different sentence types can be used for effect. From this the teacher designs challenges that are one step up from what they can already do, and the children are asked to define what a simple sentence is and how to spot one. The task is designed to allow children to try to catch each other out, in mostly mixed-ability pairs. All children will demonstrate their proficiency with simple sentences first, then compound, then complex, then a mixture of all three.

There are no trick questions here, no right or wrong – simply consider the following. Which approach values:

- Growth mindset?

- Assessment for learning (AfL)?

- Practice?

- Discussion?

- Pupil involvement?

- Opportunities to reflect?

- Creativity?
- Capability over ability?
- Peer-to-peer learning?

How can you ensure challenge for all?

Will the high-attainers feel suitably motivated by using simple sentences?

Can it be done in one lesson?

Is it possible for all pupils to achieve this objective at the same rate?

How would you approach this objective?

We just want you to contemplate this for a while and we'll come back to it later.

# DIFFERENTIATION WITHOUT LIMITS

The Learning without Limits project is an ongoing collaborative set of enquiries which questions the concept of ability-based differentiation and represents a revolutionary movement in teaching.[2] The project involves teachers whose practices include the rejection of ability labelling and studies the approaches developed by these pioneering educators in order to identify the key characteristics that underpin this movement in pedagogy. The project has highlighted that teachers who have a focus on *trans-formability* rather than *ability* – and understand that the present plays a pivotal role in pupils' capacity to learn (i.e. what and how we teach our pupils now, rather than assessments of aptitude or predefined notions of talent) – are more likely to exploit learning opportunities for all and thus enable all pupils to become better learners. The drive for transformability is inspired by a belief in all pupils' entitlement to better outcomes and in learning *capacity*, irrespective of any preconceived judgements.

The idea of co-agency is one of three principles identified through the first project that, together, enabled the teachers that the project studied to translate the core idea of transformability into practice in their classrooms:

> The principle of co-agency leads teachers to choose classroom activities and experiences for their potential to increase scope for children to influence and shape the direction of learning, to make choices and take responsibility for their own learning, to learn with and from one another rather than relying mainly on the teacher's direction and input. Unlike ability-based teaching, where the onus is essentially upon the teacher to plan for differentiation of tasks, resources and outcomes, teaching informed by the principle of co-agency recognises that diversity in learning is achieved by what both teachers and young people contribute to the learning process. What young people will learn from any particular set of tasks or activities cannot be tightly pre-specified because it will reflect not just what the teacher has prepared and anticipated for their learning but also what they put in, what they bring and what they make of the learning opportunities that the teacher provides.

---

2   See Susan Hart, Annabelle Dixon, Mary Jane Drummond and Donald McIntyre, *Learning without Limits* (Maidenhead: Open University Press, 2004); Mandy Swann, Alison Peacock, Susan Hart and Mary Jane Drummond, *Creating Learning without Limits* (Maidenhead: Open University Press, 2012).

Opportunities for sustained, purposeful dialogue between teacher and learners, and between learners themselves, are also of crucial importance, for it is through talk that young people have the chance to elaborate and develop their thinking and make ideas meaningful in their own terms.[3]

So it's clear to see that the idea of co-agency emerged strongly from the project as a principle of successful learning experiences in the classroom. The scope of the Learning without Limits project continues to widen through the development of a professional network and a series of seminars, drawing in teachers from many different sectors in the UK and internationally.

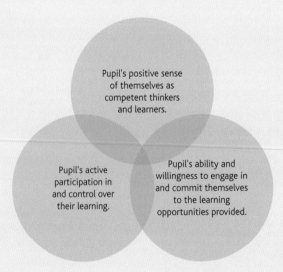

Pupil's positive sense of themselves as competent thinkers and learners.

Pupil's active participation in and control over their learning.

Pupil's ability and willingness to engage in and commit themselves to the learning opportunities provided.

Our job with differentiation is closely connected to what we have been exploring in terms of learning traits and classroom culture. Differentiation and mindset are inextricably linked. If learning tasks limit potential due to the teacher's preoccupation with predetermined levels of attainment, this denies pupils the opportunities for rich intellectual challenge and experiences of success, sets up a climate of comparison and judgement between peers and leads to a higher social value being placed on visibly

3   See http://learningwithoutlimits.educ.cam.ac.uk/about/key.html. The ideas here are synthesised from the two key texts by Hart et al. and Swann et al.

'high achievers' or 'spicy' learners, according to children like Holly. Only a fixed mindset can thrive in this environment.

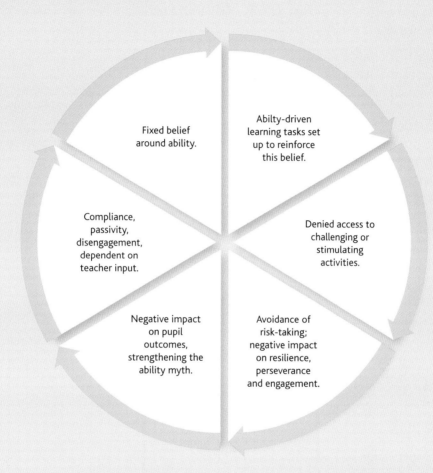

Fixed belief around ability.

Abilty-driven learning tasks set up to reinforce this belief.

Denied access to challenging or stimulating activities.

Compliance, passivity, disengagement, dependent on teacher input.

Negative impact on pupil outcomes, strengthening the ability myth.

Avoidance of risk-taking; negative impact on resilience, perseverance and engagement.

Ripe conditions for fear

Using the principle of co-agency, tasks need to be approached through a partnership between teacher and pupil, rather than through explicit teacher direction. What goes wrong in a lot of well-meaning classrooms is that the tasks themselves are not designed in a way that supports this process. Mild, medium and spicy tasks, for instance, should follow a logical journey into deepening understanding through the application of the same objective, rather than simply being three separate and unconnected activities.

Pupils can move through a set of learning tasks with a common end goal, irrespective of their starting point. The design of these tasks should take prior understanding into account and be flexible enough to help children continually reflect on whether they can aim higher.

Here are two examples of chilli challenges designed with these principles in mind. You can see the deeper knowledge needed to approach each activity. As the child progresses through the continuum of their understanding, they'll start understanding the tools they need to approach each one. In the first example, the two-chilli challenge builds on the concept introduced in the one-chilli task (you need to understand that you can make twelfths, sixths and eighteenths into equivalent fractions); however, the learners will need to use a different calculation. In the three-chilli task, the child needs to be able to construct their own group of numbers, understand deeper-level vocabulary, and know how to explain it to someone else. This is a continuum of skills built around the requirements for fraction knowledge in Year 5.

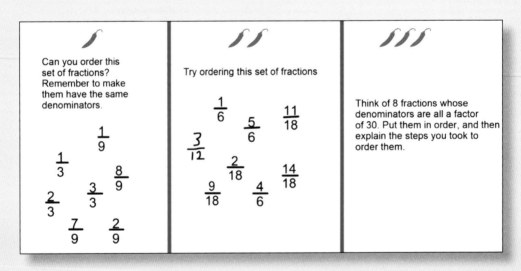

In the next example, the children are applying new understanding of the formal written method of column multiplication. The two-chilli task builds on the first by requiring understanding of the place value of thousands. In the three-chilli activity, the children will need to apply their understanding to work out the missing numbers within multiplications using numbers with up to four digits. Without the deep understanding gained through the first two tasks, the children won't have the flexible thinking required for the third. Teachers are in a strong position to adopt this principle because the current national curriculum in England is deliberately designed in a way to support this depth in understanding.

| ✎ | ✎✎ | ✎✎✎ |
|---|---|---|
| 24 x 5 | 24 x 5 | 24 x 5 |
| 243 x 2 | 2413 x 2 | 2413 x 2 |
| 186 x 3 | 1896 x 3 | 186 x ☐ = 558 |
| 201 x 4 | 2501 x 7 | ☐01 x 4 = 2404 |
| 295 x 6 | 7895 x 9 | 7295 x 6 = 43☐70 |

# MASTERY CURRICULUM

If you've been teaching for a while, you might be familiar with life before levels. Anyone who was teaching before or during the transition period will understand the collective anguish. 'I knew where I stood with levels!' we mourned. 'Why did they have to remove them? What's emerging, what's age-related, what on earth is *greater depth*?!' The struggle is real. Levels were originally brought in to define standards in primary schools, to provide absolute clarity and allow pupils to see the progress they had made against a pre-set benchmark. The introductions of SATs in 1991 and Ofsted in 1992, as a result of the 1988 Education Reform Act, muddied the waters. Slowly, schools that were focusing on standards-orientated expectations were being asked why their pupils weren't achieving *higher* than the average; in other words, good wasn't considered good enough anymore. This led to a system that promoted an inflation of standards, often to the detriment of the pupils who were whizzed through the curriculum. This pace-and-race agenda encouraged teachers to push pupils through a system of stepped levels despite weak or flimsy understanding. It wasn't uncommon for teachers to disregard the attainment and progress data that had been passed up from the previous teacher, to doubt the competency of their colleagues due to clear gaps in pupils' learning and to fear for their own sanity due to the amount of catch-up they felt they needed to implement with a new class. This was notoriously familiar for Year 6 teachers who collectively felt the burden of SATs.

Whatever your standpoint on the removal of levels, what is certain is that the rationale to remove them had 'improved outcomes for all' at the heart of its agenda. The curriculum is designed to guide children through a knowledge and skills base at an age-appropriate pace, with an emphasis on repetition, capability, confidence and mastery within the same context.[4] So we're not pushing more and more knowledge or skills at our pupils, but rather allowing the time to go over skills in a variety of ways; the space to question, think and reflect on what has been learnt; and the freedom and flexibility for pupils to explore and apply these skills in a range of contexts. This is what mastery and greater depth means, and mindset has a huge part to play.

Okay, enough of the history lesson. What does this mean for you in terms of lesson design? It's analogy time again. This one is for the bakers.

| Challenge level | Learning process | Learning phase |
|---|---|---|
| Comfort zone | When we first learn to bake something new – a sponge cake, for example – the majority of us rely on direct instruction from a recipe. We need to know the exact quantities of the ingredients and use a method to ensure we are following the right steps in the right order. This stage feels comfortable, as there is less potential to mess up if we follow clear guidelines. We're still at the practising or novice stage of our | **Working towards** <br> Novice |

---

4   Department for Education, *The National Curriculum in England: Key Stages 1 and 2 Framework Document*. Ref: DFE-00178-2013 (London: Department for Education, 2013). Available at: https://assets.publishing.service.gov.uk/government/uploads/system/uploads/attachment_data/file/425601/PRIMARY_national_curriculum.pdf.

| Challenge level | Learning process | Learning phase |
|---|---|---|
| | learning. We need to continue baking sponges to improve; we wouldn't suddenly jump to baking a tart, for instance. | |
| Learning zone | As we continue to practise, our confidence increases and perhaps we don't need to consult the ingredients list anymore or we are checking in with the recipe book less and less. We may even experiment with the quantities of ingredients and feel less rigid about the specifics – we may choose sultanas over currants, for example. It's at this stage that we start to feel assured in our capability as a baker and we feel ready to take risks in our approach. We will ask others for tips and guidance, and for feedback on the end result. We will probably get things wrong, create something we are not sure about or feel as though we need to go back to the recipe. We're independently applying what we've learnt, and we're out of our comfort zone. This is where the real learning happens. Now, we could stop here and be happy in what we've achieved, or we could explore further. | **Working at** Capable |
| Breakthrough zone | We may decide to try our baking out on other people, strangers even, and get some feedback on what's popular. From this we can start to ask questions: 'What might happen if I substitute honey for sugar or add nuts into the base?' We have the level of understanding to take bigger risks, make bigger mistakes and have more creative input. We start to make assured and accurate predictions about outcomes. At this point we can say that we can make different types of sponge cakes independently. If something goes wrong, we can work out what it is and how to fix it, and we can seek feedback on how to keep improving. We can even teach others how to bake. This is our breakthrough zone: the zone of greater depth in our understanding and proficiency. | **Greater depth** Proficient |

This analogy is informed by John Hattie's concept of the three major phases in learning, from novice to capable to proficient.[5] We believe this transition happens through practice, independent application and, finally, by having the readiness, interest and opportunity to explore further. Three-way split-ability tasks do not support this process.

The national curriculum was specifically designed to support these phases, from surface to deeper understanding, by encouraging a gradual journey through cognitive domains and not racing pupils through before they were ready or had become truly proficient.[6] The race is why it felt like learning didn't *stick* and teachers continued to question what had been going on in the children's prior learning. In *Make it Stick*, Brown, Roediger and McDaniel wrote about how simply rereading, retrying or repeating something over and over again leads to poor results when trying to really embed and retain knowledge.[7] In order to make new learning stick, they argue that we need to use retrieval techniques to recall it after a period of time. This retrieval could take the form of quizzes, questioning or application of the skill in a different context. The idea is that simple rereading doesn't force us to use the information in a way that means it will go into our long-term memories. When we try to retrieve the new skill or knowledge after a period of time has elapsed, our brains are required to get that information 'back out' – to use it, mould it and rethink it. We have already established the neural pathways, but this time we reinforce them, create new ones, and make the web of connections stronger. The reinforcement of the knowledge that the retrieval requires is a good way of using the knowledge and evolving it into long-term understanding.

Our curriculum, lesson and task designs need to support this process, and growth mindset provides the backbone. Without the mindset, pupils won't have the readiness to take part in this journey, where independent application involves getting stuck and solving problems. If we continue to model and support lower-attaining pupils using scaffold after scaffold, we aren't going to see a shift from novice to capable, let alone to proficient. We have to be bold, remove the reins and use feedback, coaching, questioning and reflection to move pupils along this journey.

---

5   John Hattie, *Visible Learning for Teachers: Maximizing Impact on Learning* (Abingdon and New York: Routledge, 2012).

6   Department for Education, *The National Curriculum in England*.

7   Peter C. Brown, Henry L. Roediger and Mark A. McDaniel, *Make it Stick: The Science of Successful Learning* (Cambridge, MA: Harvard University Press, 2014).

Joe, aged seven, has some difficulties accessing class work, and the school is in the process of applying for an education, health and care plan (EHCP). He has regular support from the class TA, and has teacher support in nearly every lesson. The impact of this support isn't enough considering the time that has been invested. During a science lesson, Joe was asked to record items around the classroom using a pre-prepared grid, and to describe their magnetic properties in the space provided. Joe sat for a while, thinking about what had been asked of him. After a pause, he asked the teacher, 'When's my help going to start?' He was so used to the scaffolding that it didn't occur to him that he could complete a task on his own. He literally sat there waiting for support. As it turns out, deliberately taking this away freed him to try it alone, and while he felt uneasy, he managed to complete the task. In hindsight, Joe had been given too much scaffolding in the hope that he would create work that was at the same level as his peers'. What was needed was for Joe to forge his own experiences – sometimes with support, but almost more importantly, sometimes without. It was during those independent episodes that he grew more. The EHCP, when it finally came to fruition, vindicated this type of support. It also decreed the provision of 'uncomfortable' tasks that Joe should experience to build his independence and resilience.

Think back to the baking analogy: if we only ever follow recipe after recipe – for fear of burning our cake or using too much flour – then we'll probably always rely on one and not have the confidence to get creative in the kitchen. We'd miss out on so much!

**COMFORT ZONE**

Novice

Practising

- Direct instruction.
- Modelling.
- Clear learning objectives.
- Success criteria.
- Repetition.
- Surface level understanding.

**LEARNING ZONE**

Capable

Independent application

- Teacher questioning.
- Gradual removal of scaffolds.
- Change one element.
- Open-ended tasks.
- Teacher feedback.
- Self-review. (I'm doing okay, I might need this next.)
- Risk-taking.

**BREAKTHROUGH ZONE**

Proficient

Further exploration

- Problem-solving.
- Application in new contexts.
- Questioning.
- Reasoning.
- Self-reflection. (I was successful here, I could've done this differently.)
- Teacher coaching.
- Peer teaching.
- Creative possibilities.

Mastery and greater depth are judged on how fluent and independent learners are in applying the skills, and they need to experience new situations in which they can try out what they've learnt. We've used the following 'How We Learn' flowchart with pupils in Key Stage 2 and they found it really useful to track where they are on the chart, particularly if they have gone wrong. It reinforces the idea of learning as a *process*; where we are in it is dependent on lots of different external factors, but all of them can be overcome.

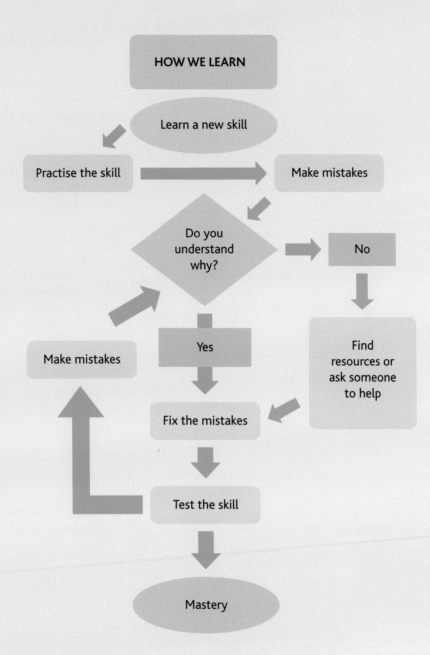

# DIFFERENTIATION

Tomlinson and Moon came up with a really clear definition of differentiation as a teacher's proactive response to learners' needs. They propose that not only is this underpinned by mindset but that it is linked to five main classroom elements: 'learning environment, curriculum, assessment, instruction, and classroom leadership and management.'[8] Handy, as we've already covered a lot of these points.

Teachers can differentiate through:

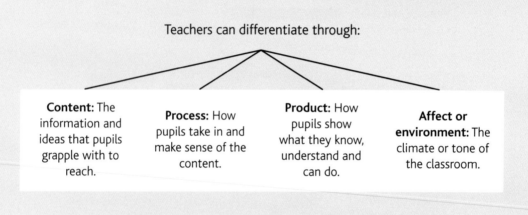

**Content:** The information and ideas that pupils grapple with to reach.

**Process:** How pupils take in and make sense of the content.

**Product:** How pupils show what they know, understand and can do.

**Affect or environment:** The climate or tone of the classroom.

According to pupils':

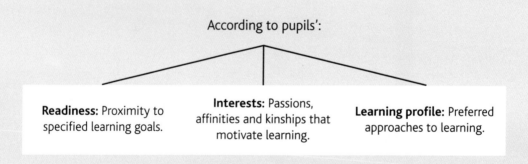

**Readiness:** Proximity to specified learning goals.

**Interests:** Passions, affinities and kinships that motivate learning.

**Learning profile:** Preferred approaches to learning.

---

8   Carol Ann Tomlinson and Tonya R. Moon, *Assessment and Student Success in a Differentiated Classroom* (Alexandria, VA: ACSD, 2013), p. 1.

We can also consider the flipside, in terms of barriers to deep levels of understanding and how to break these down.

| Nurture children's confidence through | Differentiate through |
|---|---|
| A safe classroom. | Curriculum design. |
| The journey from stuck to got-it. | Lesson structure. |
| The process of learning. | Resources and ideas. |
| Independence. | A range of assessment strategies. |
| Repetition. | Questioning and reasoning. |
| Seeing mistakes as learning opportunities. | Challenge. |
| Self-reflection. | Coaching. |
| Growth mindset. | Feedback. |

# SOLO TAXONOMY: LIKE BLOOM'S, BUT DEEPER

That first conversation about Holly was a real wake-up call for Ruchi and it was after this that she started her own research project to look into other approaches. She wanted to provide pupils with everything we've looked at so far in this chapter: access to depth of understanding irrespective of existing knowledge or skillset. Every child needed to know how capable they were, and we needed to remove the dangerous labelling that limited potential and growth. This is easier said than done when you don't know any different. Then, through her involvement with #LearningFirst – which is a community of colleagues from across education, with a shared interest in promoting an agenda for change in assessment practice – she found SOLO taxonomy. We know what you're thinking, yet *another* initiative to adopt in the classroom!

Our plea to you is this: read about it and then make up your own mind. A good place to start would be Hook.[9] We've used this model ourselves and it transformed our teaching. SOLO taxonomy is not an add-on or a new initiative, it's a model. A model that, like magic, allows you to plan and differentiate in order to support the transition from surface to deep knowledge. It's simple, straightforward and supports the learning traits of growth mindset. It guides children to ask questions that regulate their learning. Once you begin teaching using SOLO, the link with growth mindset becomes really clear, especially as pupils begin to understand that depth of learning takes time and willpower. It's a model that provides:

- A structure for learning – ideas are organised as loose, connected or extended.

- A process for learning – from one idea to several ideas to related ideas to extended ideas.

- A common language of learning – to help teachers and pupils understand the learning journey.

- A structure for assessment – through opportunities for regular peer- and self-assessment against specific learning goals.

We do need to explore the theory behind the model before we think about how best to adapt it in individual classrooms, so stay with us. SOLO stands for Structure of Observed Learning Outcomes and it describes increasingly complex levels of understanding. It's a structure that guides pupils and teachers from surface knowledge, through deep knowledge to conceptual or constructed knowledge. This is done in stages using a common framework, and the symbols make the learning outcomes clear. Like Bloom's taxonomy, SOLO is hierarchical, meaning that deeper understanding is dependent on having attained prerequisite knowledge and skills.

Biggs and Collis developed the SOLO model after conducting research into pupils' thinking and levels of competency across a range of subjects.[10] They concluded that understanding can be categorised into any one of five levels of complexity.

---

9 Pam Hook, *First Steps with SOLO Taxonomy: Applying the Model in Your Classroom* (Invercargill, NZ: Essential Resources, 2016).

10 John Biggs and Kevin Collis, *Evaluating the Quality of Learning: The SOLO Taxonomy* (New York: Academic Press, 1982).

| | SOLO language | SOLO symbol | What this means |
|---|---|---|---|
| **Working towards**<br>**Novice** | Prestructural | ○ | The pupil has not yet grasped the idea and/or needs help to start. |
| | **Surface knowledge (loose ideas)** | | |
| | Unistructural | ▯ | The pupil has one idea connected to the task and their understanding is disconnected or limited. |
| **Working at**<br>**Capable** | Multistructural | ▯▯▯ | The pupil has several connected ideas and can use reasoning to explain them. |
| | **Deep knowledge (connected ideas)** | | |
| | Relational | ⬦ | The pupil has related or linked ideas, has found patterns and can explain relationships. |

| Greater depth Proficient | Conceptual or constructed knowledge (extended ideas) | | |
|---|---|---|---|
| | Extended abstract |  | The pupil has taken the related ideas and extended them. They can use and apply these ideas in a range of contexts to predict, generalise, reflect or create. |

The SOLO model allows teachers to design differentiated learning tasks and tailor success criteria accordingly. By looking at the five levels detailed above, teachers can see where individual children – or groups of children – are, and design tasks that sit within the next level to push them on. It allows children to always be striving for the next metacognitive level, and for the teacher to provide the wealth and breadth of experiences and activities that the class need. In our teaching lives, the hardest thing can sometimes be planning for the children who are working at greater depth. With SOLO, we can use the extended abstract model to think of learning opportunities that test this competency.

The SOLO levels can be adapted for any topic in order to:

• Plan the level of learning required.

• Assess the extent to which each pupil has reached that level.

• Make decisions about the next steps for learning.

In classrooms where we have seen SOLO being used effectively, the journey of learning always relates back to these stages. This is visible enough for pupils to see that each level of understanding can be built on, that it is a cumulative process and that everyone in the learning community is on the same journey together. You may be thinking back to the chilli challenge here, and wondering whether this is actually particularly different. Well, the difference lies in how explicit you make the learning – how *visible*. With SOLO, the teacher and children share the common language of the levels and symbols.

It isn't a case of a child picking the activity they think is best – it's about all being in a tailored environment that the teacher gauges based on continuous formative assessment. It also doesn't happen in the isolation of just one task. SOLO is an environment for learning, cultivated over a sequence of lessons.

| Structured skill development and outcomes for learners | | | | | |
|---|---|---|---|---|---|
| **Stage** | Define | Identify | Describe | Explain | Apply |
| **Examples** | E.g. I need help or direction. | E.g. I will have a go at it. I can do it if directed. | E.g. I will use trial and error to find a solution. | E.g. I plan to do X because I know it will ... I know what to do and why. | E.g. I sense what to do to find the best solution. I seek feedback so I can improve. |
| **Solo level** | ○ | ▯ | ▯▯▯ | ⬍▯▯⬍ | ⬍▯▯⬍◯ |

By routinely referring to each stage of learning, it helps pupils develop this common language and understand that all learning comes from one idea that can be grown through knowledge, practice, effort and mistakes. When introducing this model to your class, it's important to connect each level of understanding with the pupils' thought processes and feelings. This provides a good basis for discussions around metacognition: knowing and understanding what they are doing, why, how they got there and where they can go next.

O

I don't know anything about this skill. I might need some help getting started.

I know something about this. I can have a go.

I can do this. I'm going to try something trickier, which means I might get stuck.

I've got it! I feel like an expert, I want to teach someone else.

I want to do more. I wonder what would happen if ...

It also reinforces the idea that learning happens as a result of direct action by the pupil. They put in the effort, use the strategies, get stuck and problem-solve, rather than just rely on luck or fixed ability. All pupils can meaningfully reflect on their progress and, using SOLO to check in as they go along, be clear on what their next steps are.

The following example was used in a Year 3 class, with inspiration coming from the open-ended style of maths investigations created by NRICH Maths.[11] Pupils had to use a systematic approach to work out a mystery number using clues. The teacher wanted to use this as a stimulus for reasoning. The lesson was chunked into small parts and children were working on mixed-ability tables. As soon as the lesson started, the children were given a problem that was similar to the main activity, but on a smaller scale. Pupils were expected to read and solve this problem together without any teacher input, while the teacher made a mini-assessment, taking careful note of common points of difficulty, who might need further support and who could be pushed further in their thinking.

---

**Learning objective: to work systematically and use known facts to derive answers.**

I'm thinking of a mystery number that is hidden in this square. Can you find my mystery number using the clues below?

| 1  | 2  | 3  | 4  | 5  | 6  |
|----|----|----|----|----|----|
| 7  | 8  | 9  | 10 | 11 | 12 |
| 13 | 14 | 15 | 16 | 17 | 18 |
| 19 | 20 | 21 | 22 | 23 | 24 |
| 25 | 26 | 27 | 28 | 29 | 30 |
| 31 | 32 | 33 | 34 | 35 | 36 |

- The number is odd. (HINT: You need to cross out all the even numbers – can you tell me why?)
- It is in the three times table.
- It is < 7 x 4.
- The tens digit in my number is even.
- The sum of the two digits is 9.

---

11  See https://nrich.maths.org/.

In case you've just had a go, the answer is 27!

The pupils were invited to share how they found the task, what helped them to get started and what made it difficult. The focus of the discussion was on the method rather than on the answer, and pupils were encouraged to explain their reasoning. The teacher also used this time to break down the learning intention so that all pupils knew which skills they would be practising.

**Learning intention:**

- To think carefully about how you will solve the problem.

- To be able to explain what you did and how you did it.

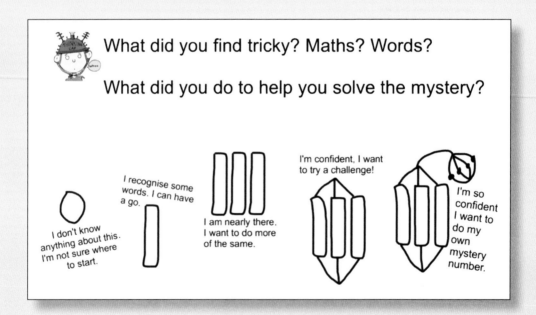

The teacher then introduced the main task, using modelling to explain the learning journey. The SOLO structure was used to help pupils understand their starting point. The pupils were encouraged to self-assess and to be active in the learning. In this particular activity, the pupils understood that everyone was either at the prestructural or unistructural level of understanding and that the only way to make progress was to have a go. Very quickly, the pupils who routinely felt as though they were 'less-able' noticed that they had moved from knowing nothing to knowing something, and this increased their confidence levels. On the flip side, the 'more-able', those who generally had fixed mindsets and always wanted to race to the end of a task or pick the hard option to prove themselves, quickly realised that they had to start in the same place as everyone else. They needed to build on each level of learning in order to progress.

With the main activity designed around everyone moving in the same direction together, it created an atmosphere of collaboration. Pupils shared ideas and engaged in maths talk. The teacher was able to direct support appropriately, given their initial assessment. The teacher worked with children who struggled with the first activity and used questioning to elicit responses.

What's interesting about this type of problem is that pupils can get to the answer quite quickly. However, the real learning takes place afterwards, at the reasoning stage. The lesson was stopped after 15 minutes or so, to check in with pupils and make sure that everyone had the answer they needed in order to move on. The teacher used the SOLO map to guide children to reflect on where they thought they were. Through focused questioning, the teacher quickly reassessed how to direct the teaching for each pupil and even used pupils' self-assessments to build success criteria.

I'm thinking of a number. Can you find my number in the grid below? Use my clues to help you.

| 0 | 1 | 2 | 3 | 4 | 5 | 6 | 7 | 8 | 9 |
|---|---|---|---|---|---|---|---|---|---|
| 10 | 11 | 12 | 13 | 14 | 15 | 16 | 17 | 18 | 19 |
| 20 | 21 | 22 | 23 | 24 | 25 | 26 | 27 | 28 | 29 |
| 30 | 31 | 32 | 33 | 34 | 35 | 36 | 37 | 38 | 39 |
| 40 | 41 | 42 | 43 | 44 | 45 | 46 | 47 | 48 | 49 |
| 50 | 51 | 52 | 53 | 54 | 55 | 56 | 57 | 58 | 59 |
| 60 | 61 | 62 | 63 | 64 | 65 | 66 | 67 | 68 | 69 |
| 70 | 71 | 72 | 73 | 74 | 75 | 76 | 77 | 78 | 79 |
| 80 | 81 | 82 | 83 | 84 | 85 | 86 | 87 | 88 | 89 |
| 90 | 91 | 92 | 93 | 94 | 95 | 96 | 97 | 98 | 99 |

| Solve the mystery using the clues below | Think carefully and describe how you solved the problem | Explain your method to show your understanding |
|---|---|---|
| ○ | ▯▯▯ | ⬖ |
| <ul><li>My mystery number is > 3 x 3.</li><li>My number **is not** a multiple of 10.</li><li>My number **is** a multiple of 7.</li><li>My number is odd.</li><li>My number **is not** a multiple of 11.</li><li>My number is < 200</li><li>The ones digit is greater than the tens digit.</li><li>The tens digit is odd.</li></ul><br>HINT: Go to the clues you understand first. Then try the others. You can do it!<br>HINT: > means 'greater than'<br>< means 'less than' | Four of the clues are true but do nothing to help you find my number.<br>Four of the clues are really important and will help you find it.<br>Sort the clues into two groups: 'clues you must have' and 'clues you don't need'. Be ready to explain how you sorted them. | When you have found the clues you must have, can you explain **why** they are the most important clues?<br>Answer these questions to help you explain:<ul><li>Which is a good clue to start with? Why?</li><li>Are there any clues that don't get rid of any numbers?</li><li>Which clue is the most useful?</li><li>Which clue helps you at the end?</li></ul> |

The answer to this one is 35.

The expectation was that everyone would make it to the 'explain' stage of the problem, and some pupils would take this even further. For those pupils, the teacher prepared another task that allowed them to consolidate their learning to create their own mystery number problem and design carefully crafted clues. This task required further thought and analysis. When they were given the freedom to create, clusters of pupils who were at the same point in their learning naturally gravitated towards each other to form mini working parties. This type of advancing task allows for peer collaboration and talk.

Learning objective: To work systematically and use known facts to derive answers.

**GOT-IT MEGA CHALLENGE:** Use the 100 square to create your own puzzle with clues.

Think about which challenge you want to go for.

| Swimming on the surface | Main challenge | Swimming deep |
|---|---|---|
| Give your partner a list of clues to help them find the number. | Try to create four clues that you must use and four clues that are not needed to find the answer. | Use some of the maths vocabulary below to make your partner really think about the numbers they have to eliminate. |
| **Maths vocabulary** | | |
| Odd<br>Even<br>Greater than ><br>Less than < | Ones<br>Tens | Multiple of<br>Sum of |

For pupils with SEN, the task was adapted to ensure that the same reasoning skills were being used but in an accessible context. These pupils were also challenged to create their own problem, ensuring that progression was possible. The main differences were that the clues focused on more than and less than (< and >) and that the number was between 1 and 10. Adult support was also given in the first instance and then slowly withdrawn when the children had started to put the idea into action.

By the end of the lesson, pupils were able to articulate their progress using the SOLO framework. *All* pupils were able to see how they had moved on in their learning and reflective discussions took place between learners and their teacher. Once embedded through repeated use, the common language of SOLO helps pupils to see the process from 'I'm not sure about this' to 'I can link my ideas to see the big picture', and some may even go beyond and create links with other ideas. In this model, learning is endless and never capped.

## SOLO in practice

In terms of mindset, SOLO shows pupils that learning is the result of effort and strategies, not a fixed ability or *looking smart*. It shows a clear learning progression and next step for every learner. Have a look at the table that follows. Here we've used Bloom's taxonomy, which provides a framework for higher-order thinking, to classify verbs that can help shape learning outcomes for each stage. As with Bloom's, a hierarchy like SOLO can assist teachers in designing tasks, crafting questions and providing feedback on work.

| Surface understanding | | Deep understanding | |
|---|---|---|---|
| UNISTRUCTURAL Making simple connections | MULTISTRUCTURAL Solving problems at a surface level | RELATIONAL Inquiry and application | EXTENDED ABSTRACT Bringing in another skill, questioning or investigating |
| Identify | Describe | Inquire | Imagine |
| Define | List | Explain | Elaborate |
| Recognise | Outline | Organise | Initiate |

| | | | |
|---|---|---|---|
| Quote | Combine | Find | Create |
| Name | Follow | Question | Visualise |
| Recall | Solve | Analyse | Generalise |
| Match | List | Compare and contrast | Predict |
| | | Summarise | Justify |
| | | Evaluate | Construct |
| | | | Perform |
| | | | Theorise |
| | | | Prove |
| | | | Argue |
| | | | Assess |

Remember Teacher A and B from earlier? The ones who were trying to design a task around simple, compound and complex sentences? We did promise we'd come back to it, so let's take the SOLO model and try to map out the structure and process of the learning. The first thing we need to think about is the *big idea*. What exactly is it that we need the pupils to understand? The task will need to be designed around this big idea in order to create a progressive learning journey and challenges that are one step up from what the pupils can already do.

In this example, we need pupils to define, identify, describe, find, evaluate and create their own simple, complex and compound sentences. This is working at the expected standard. If pupils can then use their understanding of sentence types to create specific effects in their writing – and justify how – then we can confidently assess these pupils as working at a greater depth. In order for the pupils to achieve this level of thinking, they need to master simple and compound sentences and feel confident in using them before they can move on.

| Prestructural level | **Define** and **identify** a simple sentence. |
|---|---|
| Unistructural level | **Identify** what it is and what it is not.<br>e.g. *I have a brown dog, too.*<br>**Recognise** simple sentences in texts. |
| Multistructural level | **List** all the features of a simple sentence, creating a toolkit for *how* to identify or write one.<br>**Solve** through investigation. What happens if you add another verb, noun or adjective.<br>e.g. Is '*The brown, shaggy dog jumped*' still a simple sentence? |
| Relational level | **Find** simple sentences in texts and **explain** how you know that they are simple.<br>**Compare** and **contrast** them to a compound sentence. (What do you notice? What is the same and what is different?)<br>**Evaluate** what a compound sentence is. Create a toolkit for how to identify or write one. Find as many rules as you can. |
| Extended abstract level | **Justify** or **argue** to **prove** what is compound, simple or neither, using examples.<br>**Predict** what a complex sentence is, using what you know.<br>**Elaborate** on what you know about all three types of sentence. Spot patterns to create a toolkit.<br>**Theorise** the author's purpose in using all three types of sentence.<br>**Create** your own piece of writing using different types of sentences and **assess** the effect this has on the reader. |

In this learning journey a typical cohort of pupils may have a wide range of starting points, and through the initial assessment by the class teacher – usually during a fairly open-ended task – the pupils will be able to determine the right differentiated task, with the teacher's support.

When you break the learning down like this it suddenly becomes so clear that the objectives must also be broken down before meaningful learning can take place. If you think you can teach sentence types in one lesson using three 'levelled' worksheets, think again! There's a lot of work involved here – it takes time, effort and a degree of scaffolding at the beginning. Once pupils get to the relational stage of their learning, those scaffolds can be removed and more reflective discussions should start happening in the classroom. Underpinning this is metacognition. Children can use the SOLO levels to:

- Feed-up: where am I going? What are the goals? What is the end result that I want to achieve?

- Feed-back: how am I going? (At this point, timely and pinpointed teacher responses to the work are useful, allowing the child to know what needs to happen next, and what might need to change.)

- Feed-forward: where to next? In response to the feedback from my teacher, what is the next small step going to look like? What do I need to change so that I can get closer to that end result?[12]

Here's something you can try in your classroom tomorrow, particularly if you're starting a new topic or introducing a new concept. This can be adapted by year group and for EYFS or Key Stage 1, you can provide words or pictures. Be sure to throw in a few red herrings so that pupils have to think carefully when grouping. At the extended abstract stage, younger pupils can draw their own idea to add to the existing collection.

---

12  Douglas, Fisher and Nancy Frey, Feed Up, Back, Forward, *Educational Leadership*, 67(3) (2009): 20–25. Available at: http://www.ascd.org/publications/educational-leadership/nov09/vol67/num03/Feed-Up,-Back,-Forward.aspx.

### Unistructural

Write one fact about a topic on a sticky note.

### Multistructural

Now stick your sticky note on the board. While you're there, have a look at everyone else's points. Think about any you agree or disagree with, and any that you feel you could add to.

### Relational

In pairs, come to the board and pick three sticky notes that have something in common. For example, the same theme, idea, genre, setting, material, meaning, etc.

Combine your points into a short paragraph and be ready to discuss and justify your choices.

### Extended abstract

Add at least one sentence to your paragraph that begins with either of the following: 'I think it is really effective because ...' or 'This made me think about ...'

When we talk to teachers about SOLO, the consensus is that getting to the extended abstract is a big jump for a lot of pupils. It both requires and develops abstract and critical thinking and higher-order questioning skills. At this stage pupils need to start asking:

- What would happen if ...?

- What can I link this to?

- How can I apply this skill?

- How will I remember and teach this skill?

This also requires higher levels of questioning from the teacher. When you plan your lessons in this way, you can start to match the level of your questions to the critical thinking level of the task. Bloom's is a really good place to start when crafting questions to match your learning objective and task level. Pam Hook has developed a whole world of resources around SOLO, including rubrics, posters, stamps, stickers – for noting rather than celebrating: think praise and motivation – and actions that will really help any teacher who wants to fully invest in the SOLO model.[13] Hook is an advocate of the See Think Wonder routine, which is used for making meaning.[14]

Pupils are asked:

- What do you see? (Multistructural outcome – bringing in ideas.)

- What do you think about that? (Relational outcome – connecting ideas.)

- What does it make you wonder? (Extended abstract – extending ideas.)

We have developed a simple two-part scaffold to help pupils construct questions and develop their thinking at the beginning of a new topic. The vocabulary can be adapted to suit and questions can be modelled to support.

| Anglo-Saxon | Christianity | illuminated text | conquer | Pagan |
| --- | --- | --- | --- | --- |
| settlement | Viking | loot | missionary | barbarian |
| Picts | source | nobleman/ woman | ceorl | mint |

13 She has written a series of three books with Liz McNeil about SOLO taxonomy and making meaning. Details can be found in the references and further reading section.

14 See http://www.visiblethinkingpz.org/VisibleThinking_html_files/03_ThinkingRoutines/03c_Core_routines/SeeThinkWonder/SeeThinkWonder_Routine.html.

| Question stems | | |
|---|---|---|
| What ...? | Why ...? | How ...? |
| When ...? | Will ...? | Does/Did ...? |
| Who ...? | Is ...? | Can ...? |
| | | Which ...? |

The following table can then be copied by the pupils into their books, and they can use the question stems and the word bank to help them complete it.

| Vocabulary that I definitely know and can explain. | Vocabulary that I think I know but I'm not sure. | Questions that I could ask to help me find out. | Vocabulary that I want to explore and questions that I could ask to help me. |
|---|---|---|---|
| | | | |

In our own classrooms, SOLO provided a starting point for planning and for all our differentiated learning tasks. Over the year our pupils developed a proactive, can-do approach to most tasks. The fact that they could see their progress spurred them on and reinforced all the ongoing messages about growth mindset traits. We came a long way from the fixed mindset around 'mild' ability and instead pupils were telling us:

SOLO can help us design tasks to support the shift from working at the expected standard to greater depth (capable to proficient). If we apply this to our Challenge Ocean analogy, depth of learning comes from the mindset and confidence to 'go deep', both in learning and in the teaching of each new skill.

When differentiating a task, it might be useful to use the following model as well as SOLO to consider how your teaching style within each learning stage impacts differentiation, challenge and outcome. It is similar in shape to James Nottingham's learning pit, but here we're looking at the skills needed to move forward at each stage of the journey.[15] Making these explicit is useful for teachers when planning, as we've just seen with the SOLO levels. Connecting each skill to each stage of the journey helps pupils to understand the metacognitions they'll have been talking about in class. With this model, the stages that the pupils are going through are explicit, while Nottingham's learning pit references the feelings that are associated with being stuck. You could develop our model further by attaching a learning objective to each stage of Challenge Ocean. It's a good reference point when you want to make the learning journey really clear for the pupils. You could even use a visual of Challenge Ocean at the start of a new unit to illustrate where the learning will get deep, and therefore feel harder. By showing the children that they can use the tools from the survival kit, you'll teach them that they'll be able to keep going.

---

15 James Nottingham, *The Learning Challenge: How to Guide Your Students Through the Learning Pit to Achieve Deeper Understanding* (Thousand Oaks, CA: Corwin Publishing, 2017).

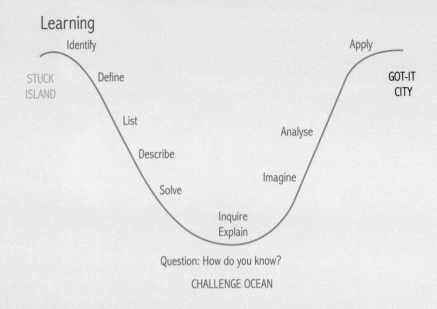

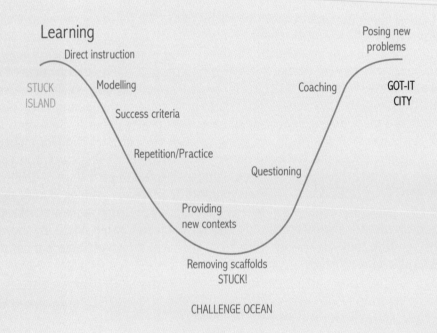

## SOLO summary

Why it works:

- Children are not capped by ability.

- It provides a model of differentiation by challenge.

- Children can communicate their feedback about the learning easily with signals, symbols and key phrases.

- Learners can see how their effort and hard work can pay off within a lesson.

- SOLO can be structured for any learning task, meaning every child has the potential to become a master of a skill.

- Learning becomes fluid and accessible to all.

- Overconfident learners (those with fixed mindsets) can see that there is always a process to learning; starting points may vary but extra effort will pay off.

- Teachers and pupils understand the journey and the process, and this creates a learning community of relatedness.

- As it is learner-centred and accessible to all, this helps remove the fear.

- It helps set clear goals and criteria for self- and peer-assessment.

- It develops self-regulation and metacognition.

- Self-autonomy creates confident learners.

- It supports the development of growth mindset and successful learning traits.

# AND FINALLY ...

Take a breath, we've covered a lot in this chapter. We wanted to conclude by bringing us back to those core pedagogical principles defined by the Learning without Limits project in order to secure successful learning outcomes for *all* pupils. Out with ability labelling and in with co-agency!

**Unpredictability:** Keep an open mind, know that attainment was assessed in the past, but it does not determine the future. Outcomes should not be predetermined.

**Trust:** Children want to learn and will engage if the conditions are right: high expectations for all, never capped by 'ability', the teacher keeps looking for the right tool to unlock their potential.

**Pedagogical principles**

**Co-agency:** Active engagement, teachers and pupils work together with a collective sense of responsibility. The culture recognises the importance of dialogue, feedback and feedforward.

**Everybody:** Entitlement and belonging, relatedness, all pupils have the potential to improve and get better at learning.

And just to be sure you don't get lost in a well-intended world of mild, medium and spicy inadvertent ability grouping, here are our final top tips for pupil-driven differentiation:

| Try to ... | Remember that pupil-driven differentiation does not ... |
|---|---|
| Make conversations about pupil voice. | Result in a free-for-all. |
| Rely on communication and strong teacher–pupil relationships. | Require you to plan something different for every pupil. |
| Strive for an autonomous classroom. | Rely on a single form of assessment. |
| Incorporate flexibility within structure. | Just give pupils a choice. |
| Provide clear learning intentions, success criteria and checks for understanding. | Mean you just give pupils different work. |
| | Take too much time to implement. |

| | |
|---|---|
| Use multiple approaches for assessment and evidence. | Produce pupils who feel entitled. |
| Honour pupil readiness. | |
| Allow and accept that pupils progress at different rates. | |
| Offer authentic learning opportunities which promote pupil ownership. | |
| Celebrate pupils' feelings of success. | |

# CLASS SURVIVAL KIT

With so much to think about, incorporating these ideas can feel really daunting, particularly if you are newly qualified. In the spirit of having a go and taking risks, here's a survival kit for teachers, to help you conquer Challenge Ocean in your classroom practice.

| **Lifeguard**  | Talk to colleagues within your team or phase, or partner up with other schools who are already delivering the curriculum in this way. Whatever you do, collaborate! |
|---|---|
| **Rubber ring**  | Think about what resources can help you. Online resources: <br> • Chris Quigley – http://www.chrisquigley.co.uk/. <br> • Maths Hub – http://www.mathshubs.org.uk/. <br> • NCETM mastery documents – https://www.ncetm.org.uk/resources/. |

- CLPE reading scales – https://clpe.org.uk/library-and-resources/reading-and-writing-scales.

Books:

- You'll find plenty of useful resources in the references and further reading section.
- For this area, we'd particularly recommend John Hattie's and Pam Hook's work.

**Compass**

Use Bloom's taxonomy to help you plan the learning journey. Use SOLO taxonomy to structure the way in which you want to encourage your pupils to think.

**Lifejacket**

These approaches take time and thought. Don't just reuse last year's planning; it won't have incorporated *your* new learning. By all means use it as a jumping-off point – if the curriculum content hasn't changed – but use the structures from this chapter to help you define your own new ideas and craft the vehicle of your teaching alongside them.

**Goggles**

Read your questions and differentiated resources back.

Do your questions and resources elicit deep thinking?

Is there an opportunity for pupils to get stuck? If so, great!

Where will you start to remove the scaffolds to encourage deep understanding?

**Snorkel**

Breathe! Remember that you can't achieve everything at once. Try this approach in one subject area first. Deep, structural changes to the curriculum can only happen when the whole-school community comes together. You have the power to do your bit, so start there.

# Chapter 8

# FEEDBACK, MARKING AND PRAISE

## MOTIVATION IS WHAT YOU NEED

Everyone's heard about Google's innovative culture and working practices. They seem to have cracked the balance between happy workers and productivity. So, what do they do differently? Google took Edward Deci's research into intrinsic and extrinsic motivation and shook up the traditional ways of rewarding their employees.[1] Deci found that, in the long term, external motivators – such as bonuses, additional perks and non-specific praise – actually had a negative effect on employees' motivation. While it did give an immediate boost to productivity, this was short lived, and the rewards became the norm; employees came to expect it and so didn't necessarily work harder for it. Over time, recognition and bonuses began to lose their value. Initial employee encouragement (leading to better engagement, more work, and larger output), soon began to wane. The employees lost interest because the motivation was based on gimmick, not long-term, psychologically sound personal growth.

Deci found that the biggest influence on highly skilled workers' motivation was being trusted to work with *autonomy*.[2] Workers became self-driven because of their desire to develop their own skills and knowledge. These ideas are tried and tested in our classrooms (and, indeed, staffrooms). Extrinsic motivation only goes so far in our quest to develop brave, independent learners and our journey thus far has all been about igniting pupils' internal desire to achieve and succeed. In the case of Google, yes, they do still offer the usual benefits such as health schemes, holiday packages and monetary incentives, but they also understand that happy employees are those who are given some freedoms and flexibilities at work. Remember back in Chapter 6 when we discussed their 20% time concept? A whole day a week to tinker, explore, question and wonder. They also show their employees greater trust, whether this be through

---

1   Richard M. Ryan and Edward L. Deci, When Rewards Compete with Nature: The Undermining of Intrinsic Motivation and Self-Regulation. In Carol Sansone and Judith M. Harackiewicz (eds), *Intrinsic and Extrinsic Motivation: The Search for Optimal Motivation and Performance* (San Diego, CA: Academic Press, 2000), pp. 13–54.
2   Deci with Flaste, *Why We Do What We Do*.

discretion over their working hours or giving them a number of channels through which they can communicate their ideas. In turn, employees use this time and space to not only get their work done but actually surpass expectations in terms of output and productivity. Autonomy goes a long way.

So, think about your classroom now. What drives your pupils? Recognition from you? Recognition from peers? Self-pride? A tick in their books? A certificate from the head teacher? Applause in assembly? Be careful here, we asked what drives them, not what makes them feel good. There *is* a subtle difference, but the effect can be huge. If your classroom is like Google, where is the autonomy and the trust? Do you dangle external carrots through rewards; hollow praise, (*Well done! Clever girl! Good boy! Look how much you've done!*), certificates, raffle tickets, marbles in a jar, stickers, etc.? In the long term, what impact does this have on the mindset and learning traits of your pupils? Does it actually work? Could it be doing more damage than good?

# PROCESS PRAISE

To explore this point, there's a little boy we'd like you to get to know. We bet there's a character like him in every classroom.

James is a five-year-old boy who has been told he is 'bright' for as long as he can remember. His mum's a teacher and is very proud of him. You can tell by the way he talks about stories, games and his life experiences that his parents encourage him and give him every opportunity to learn.

In class he always puts his hand up – he's your go-to child if you need a role model or responsible errand-runner. You may even have had him labelled *high ability* (pre-2017 – old money) or greater depth/working above/secure/above age-related expectations – the list goes on.

His book is full of ticks and smiley faces. He takes his many stickers home and collects them on his bedstead. He always plays by the rules, and always does what is expected of him. When the electronic voice on the supermarket travelator says, 'Hold onto the handrail', he holds onto the handrail. This is how he measures his success. He soaks up praise, because he's so used to it. After observing James for a while, you start to wonder if he's working hard for the sticker, for his parents or to impress you, rather than to satisfy his own love of learning. Here we hit the problem.

James was once at a birthday party where the children were invited to play a game of limbo. James was excited. He went through the first few rounds, making sure he bent backwards exactly as he'd been shown, all the time watching some of the other children bend forward and crawl through. Disaster! The third round saw him knock the pole down, due to his rule-abiding awkward manoeuvre. He dissolved into tears and hid under a table, unwilling to try again or rejoin the game. This was new territory; he was used to success and didn't have the resilience to think, 'Oh well, I'll just give it another go!' Suddenly, any subsequent praise was inauthentic and meaningless – it didn't motivate him. He rejected the offer of a medal at the end, saying that he knocked the bar off so didn't deserve it.

Had James experienced 'failure' in a supported, growth-mindset-led environment, the outcome of this experience could have been very different. We want our learners to value the process of learning, rather than just the outcome. Our feedback, systems and language of praise are the vital keys to achieving this. When the praise we provide encourages children to focus on how well they are doing, they come to understand their successes by the reward. Children look to the adult for approval and this develops a dependency on validation. For James, not only will a reliance on adult praise or external reward have little effect on his achievement, it could actually disengage him from learning and effort.

James' fixed mindset tells him:

- Look smart at all costs. If you appear 'dumb' it must mean you're not good enough.

- Success should come naturally, because if you have to work it must mean you're not good enough.

- Hide mistakes and run from difficulty. If you're wrong or it's difficult, it must mean you're not good enough.

Once James' teacher recognises this, she needs to:

- Shift her language from *intelligence praise* – clever boy, you got them all right, you're really good at maths – to *process praise* – praising effort, struggle, strategies and choices, and the learning this creates, rather than an end result.

- Remove the stickers as a 'trophy of outcome'. Unless a child can go through their book and attribute every sticker to a journey of learning, what are they gaining? James shows us that the outcome may be the opposite of what we intended.

- Describe rather than evaluate what she sees, making explicit reference to traits that support a growth mindset (effort, resilience, challenge, collaboration, higher-order thinking, etc.).

- Involve James in reflecting on his own work and assessing the successes and failures.

For so long teachers have used praise as the number-one tool for reinforcing desired behaviours, whether this is in the form of proximity praise, positive reinforcement through praise or praising the behaviour we want to see (and ignoring the ones we don't). Sometimes it seems as though we are praising pupils simply for being at school: 'Thank you for coming to school today, Ravi', 'Well done for opening your book and picking up your pencil, Lottie.' Is this really necessary? Encouragement and support are not synonymous with praise and it is perfectly possible to nurture children's confidence and self-esteem without making praise the prize.

| Praise problem | Message given |
|---|---|
| Children taking the easy route to ensure success. | *Clever* people can 'just do it' and their work is always ticked. |
| Seeing feedback as direct criticism. | Everyone's always told me that I'm clever – why aren't you telling me the same thing? |

| Praise problem | Message given |
|---|---|
| Becoming a people-pleaser. | The purpose of my learning is to make others happy with me and my work. It makes me feel valued. |
| Developing anxiety about future failure. | If I don't always get things right, what will happen? This uncertainty is something to worry about. |
| Praising mediocrity under the guise of raising self-esteem. | If the teacher is pleased with what I've already done, there's no need to challenge myself any further. |

Okay, so you know what can go wrong, you've thrown out the stickers, and you're thinking about process praise. Here's how to help the Jameses in your classroom.

We can give you some stock phrases to start using with your pupils, but the point is that you need to recognise your own praise style and be mindful of *what* you are praising. Once you start noticing, you can begin to rewire your approach to praise and feedback. This is what will have a direct impact on mindset. When you say something like, 'Wow! You did that so quickly, well done', you are inadvertently setting the expectation that unless every piece of work is completed as fast, you won't be impressed. This is exactly where the fear starts to emerge and, before you've even realised, you have pupils in your class who are worried about not meeting your expectations. They take the easy route and stay in their comfort zone on Stuck Island. They choose something they can do quickly, they finish it, they get praised for it.

Of course, there is a place for you to praise your pupils when you are proud of them or when they have achieved something and they need to feel noticed and recognised – this helps build trust and engagement between teachers and pupils, which is really important. Our message is about understanding the importance of feedback in learning and recognising when ill-considered praise might dilute this process.

Have a look at some of the feedback phrases displayed on pages 155–156. How could you start introducing them into your daily practice? Consider this order of events:

Pick a bank of growth mindset phrases that you want to hear your pupils using and display them in your classroom.

Start modelling the language verbally during whole-class teaching.

In addition to modelling the phrases, begin to encourage pupils to use the phrases in paired talk and group work.

Pupils begin to self-reflect and use the taught language.

Pupils begin to respond to your feedback using the phrases. Pupils know and understand that feedback leads to continued improvement. They develop *agency*.

Once this language is secure and second nature, begin to develop bespoke phrases that fit the needs of the pupils in your class.

You're doing so much better — you're really improving and growing in ____.

I can see you've used ____ here. Has it been successful? Why do you think that?

Wow — you're really improving! I can see you've been practising. Try ____ next.

You've struggled today, that means you must be in the learning zone. You should feel proud that you didn't give up.

You've learnt so much — I'm really glad you asked those questions.

You've worked hard so far; do you think you can keep going? Have a go at ____.

Be proud of those mistakes — now you know what you need to practise.

When you feel this is hard, that's the exact time to remember you can get better. Keep diving!

You did that so quickly — I'm sorry you were given something you could already do. Let's try something different that you'll be able to learn from.

If you're not getting stuck, it means you can already do it. If you can already do it, then you're not learning.

I can see you've put effort in today, because ____.

You have achieved ___. How do you feel? What helped you get there?

I'm glad you made that mistake, because now you can tell us what you learnt from it so we can learn too.

Do you know where you went wrong? Great — you can try something different next time.

I noticed you trying new things today, what do you think helped you to stay on track?

## Task

**Lesson focus**

| Resilience | Challenge | Higher-order thinking | Effort | Collaboration | Explicit growth mindset teaching |
|---|---|---|---|---|---|

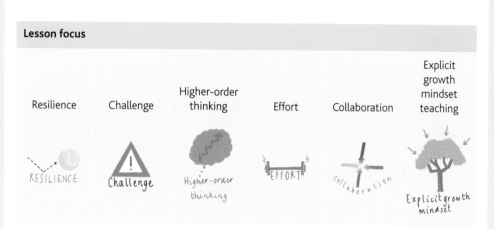

Create your own feedback phrases based on the learning traits in the key above and begin using them when giving verbal feedback, ensuring you are explicit about when and how pupils have shown the traits. When you are marking books, simplify the symbols and use them as part of your routine marking, drawing attention to where the pupils have demonstrated the traits.

Intrinsic motivation doesn't come easily to everyone – children or adults. You will come across pupils who may have become disaffected or find learning within the confines of a classroom hard to manage. Yes, ideally all our pupils will want to learn because it comes from somewhere deep inside their psyche. However, the reality is very different and we're sure you can think of pupils who you worry about. They are reliant on rewards and we're not suggesting that the change happens quickly or easily. What we can tell you is that if you start small and develop it at a comfortable pace, you will see a change – but the change starts with you. If you implement the ideas we have discussed in this book so far, your pupils will go on that journey with you, but it must be delivered with conviction.

From Deci's research around employee motivation that we discussed at the start of this chapter, we have identified four key factors in developing intrinsic motivation: meaningfulness, progress, choice and competence.

| Meaningfulness | Choice |
|---|---|
| **Agency:** Pupils developing metacognition in order to seek meaning and act with purpose. | **Autonomy:** Providing tools and opportunities for pupils to make their own decisions. |
| **Safe classroom:** Pupils using the environment and the tools within it to develop learning habits. | **Trust:** Giving pupils the confidence to try things out for themselves first. |
| **Identifying passions:** Finding out what sparks pupils' interests. | **Security:** Eliminating the fear of making mistakes. |
| **Building a community:** Giving pupils a voice in the classroom. | **Clear goals:** Understanding personal targets for growth and why. |
| **Purpose:** Connecting learning to tangible and relatable outcomes and feelings. | |
| **Voice:** Encouraging and respecting pupils' perspectives. Using higher-level questioning to challenge thinking. | |

| Progress | Competence |
|---|---|
| **Collaboration:** Encouraging pupils to share expertise and learn from each other. | **Knowledge:** Providing the right questions to scaffold learning. |
| **Milestones:** Providing reference points to mark accomplishments on the learning journey. | **Feedback:** Recognising effort and achievement and giving direction when needed. |
| **Celebrations:** Recognising and sharing personal and community milestones with others. | **Self-assessment:** Ensuring pupils recognise individual accomplishments and how they got there. |

**Visible improvement:** Clearly defining steps to success so pupils can measure their own.

**Challenge:** Allowing all pupils to feel stretched.

**Clarity:** Giving feedback in ways that provide scaffolding for pupils to self-edit and correct.

# FEEDBACK AND POLICY

Approaches to marking and feedback have become a bit of a minefield, with some schools completely overhauling their policies, some removing written feedback altogether and some standing strong with colour-coded target marking. It's difficult to challenge policy if you're not at the top and, actually, we're talking boots on the ground stuff here. Policy shouldn't make too much difference. Put simply, if you are following the principles outlined in this book – using formative assessment in your classroom and involving your pupils in the process – you will naturally be using feedback and feedforward techniques as part of that process.

Of course, we shouldn't confuse marking with feedback – they are not always the same thing. We feel that the word 'marking' puts the onus on the teachers – what they're writing in books for the children to read and, hopefully, respond to. But this starts a lengthy process of writing a comment, asking the children to respond, reading their response, responding to their response, and so on. While the comment might give the child ideas on how to improve, it is rare that written 'marking' gives timely, constructive *feedback* in the moment that it's needed. They can't understand it and apply it to the learning of that moment; with feedback, however, they can. Ask yourself, are the words or symbols that I add to this piece of work going to make an impact on the child's learning the next time they need to apply this skill? If the answer is no, then the dialogue should have taken the form of feedback and feedforward. In the current climate of trying to reduce unnecessary teacher workload, 'marking' can be synonymous with 'deep marking' – the requirement to correct spellings, punctuation, style, content, etc. and to add comments, praise and next steps at the end of the child's work – with the expectation that deep marking is done once, twice or three times a week. The same questions must apply: for whose benefit is the deep marking, and will it have an impact on this child's long-term learning? If the answers are senior leadership, or Ofsted, and probably not, then reconsider.

There are other ways to feed back to your children, as we have discussed. Dialogic, visible teaching and learning are the winners here. What really matters is how you interact with learners during the learning, not afterwards. Are you prompting and guiding their thinking or doing it for them? Do pupils have the time and freedom to think about where to go next and to explore? Do pupils have the time to respond to your feedback (be it written or verbal), and when they respond, are they expected to do it correctly the first time?

The recent interest in dedicated improvement and reflection time (DIRT) has been considerable. Pupils are given a slot of time – often in the morning during registration – to look at and respond to written marking. It sounds like a good idea in principle. But again, we urge you to consider if there is going to be a positive change in your pupils because of it. Could the time be better spent discussing the whole class' work, or going over misconceptions you have noticed? Mini-plenaries during the lesson could remove the need for DIRT, as the children are looking critically at the work they are doing there and then, and have the chance to respond to your feedback in the moment. Whether this satisfies schools' need to provide evidence of feedback is what causes the sticking point.

Most importantly, ask yourself, how can I give feedback that isn't reliant on marking?

Whatever the guidelines, effective feedback invariably:

- Happens within the lesson, when it is still relevant.

- Focuses on learning and learning objectives.

- Aims to close the gap between where pupils are in their attainment and where they could be.

- Is specific.

- Is understood by the learner.

- Is achievable there and then.

- Develops critical evaluation and thinking skills.

- Helps pupils understand what they are doing well, as well as what to try next.

- Nurtures pupils' agency rather than teachers' responsibility.

Back in Chapter 5 we looked at using questioning to elicit thinking, using the analogy of a plane in flight. This is a wonderful way to encourage your pupils to let you know how things are going. Guide them to think critically and deeply about the learning through verbal, visual or written prompts. Through your feedback, encourage deep thinking using the following strategies. You can also vary the approach, as these ideas could be discussed with a peer, filmed or recorded as a learning podcast, presented to the class, talked through with an adult, tweeted or logged on a learning wall rather than being written in books.

Now try to be a coach to another learner.

Note down what was straightforward and what was tricky. Did this surprise you?

Ask your peer to rate you!

Look at the success criteria/toolkit, where do you need to go next?

What might you need in order to get there?

What mindset traits would be useful? Explain why.

Make a mind map that demonstrates your learning. Think of ways that you can connect what you have achieved today to what you have done before and what you might do in the future.

Imagine I'm giving you a task to challenge you. What could it be? Have a go at completing it!

Try to rewrite this question to make it the right level of challenge for a learner in Reception, Year 4 or Year 7.

How could I have made this easier?

How could I have made this harder?

Try to uplevel a previous piece of work as a result of your new learning.

This is the answer. What could the question be?

Look at our learning journey. What could we do next to show our learning?

Think of some real-world examples of when you might need to use your new skill.

What was the most confusing part of this challenge?

What advice would you give yourself if you had to complete a similar task?

On a scale of 1 to 10, how would you rate your effort today? Explain!

'I learnt a lot today'. Agree or disagree? Why?

Think of a question that you have about what we have learnt that you still cannot answer.

If you were the teacher, what feedback would you give yourself about today's learning?

What did you use from the survival kit today? What could you have used?

We would encourage EYFS teachers to adapt these, which is entirely possible without 'dumbing down' just because your pupils are younger. In fact, you are at an advantage because feedback and ongoing assessment is the foundation of your practice; you are constantly observing, questioning, supporting, guiding and modelling while simultaneously encouraging curiosity and independence. The trick is to start making the process more explicit. If pupils can recognise their own effort and hard work without a praise intervention when they are in the early years, they are less likely to develop a dependency on this later in their education. So our formula for success looks something like this:

Removal of performance praise = focused feedback = agency = relatedness = less fear = growth mindset = metacognition = lifelong learners.

Phew ... mission accomplished! Well, nearly ...

Chapter 9

# CLASSROOM ASSESSMENT

In your day-to-day teaching, how reliant are you on tests? We don't mean SATs-style mocks – desks apart, silence and seriousness – but weekly quiz-style tests on spelling, times tables, grammar, punctuation and the like. What would happen if you didn't do this anymore?

Now hang on, we know what you're thinking, 'You can't start taking tests away, pupils need to experience that pressure and develop their focus and speed. It's good practice, it's important to build memory, increase fluency, etc.' Don't worry, we're not going to suggest removing tests, but we are going to go back to the original question: how *reliant* are you on tests? Think about those weekly spellings and tables you test on a Friday, what do you do with the results? Do they function as a *diagnostic* assessment? If they do, well done. If they don't, is it time to reconsider that RAG (red for 'not attained', amber for 'getting there' and green for 'achieved it') spreadsheet that you created to remind you of your pupils' strengths and weaknesses? If your pupils get 7 out of 10 on their spellings, do they know what this means? Is a 7 low, middle or high? Is the focus on the score or on improving the errors? This is the stuff that matters to them, this is the first thing their parents will ask when they get home. This is what contributes to fixed ideas about ability. 10 out of 10 means clever and anything lower is a 'try harder next time'. This is what contributes to the fear. Is this the best way to assess learning?

We want to share a recent experience of testing that, for us, highlighted the fixed nature of this sort of practice. Ruchi worked with a school which gave pupils a weekly times table challenge alongside a levelled calculation challenge. This happened from Year 1 up to Year 6. Both challenges were timed, and the pupils enjoyed them, excitedly marking their times tables to see how many they got right and eagerly awaiting the results of their calculation challenge to see if they had moved up a level (they weren't trusted to self-mark this, of course). Week after week, Ruchi noticed the same pattern in every single year group: some children were driven by moving up to the next level and getting as many calculations right as possible. Within six months some pupils had moved up six levels, while some had remained where they were. Some pupils had stayed at the same level for the past 6 months. Needless to say, they didn't think very highly of themselves as mathematicians. Maths wasn't for them, it was for the others.

What baffled Ruchi even further was that, in some classrooms, the tests were not reflective of anything the pupils had learnt that week. Some teachers were repeatedly presenting pupils with questions they struggled with, somehow expecting (or hoping) that their scores would increase. On top of this, teachers and TAs were spending time preparing 60 tests per class per week (two tests each for 30 children), checking or marking the results and then noting them down on a spreadsheet. As far as Ruchi was aware, no one ever really looked at these results. Confused about what the value of these assessments was, Ruchi asked, what is the point of these tests?

'The children love them.'

'They feel good when they get things right.'

'They really like seeing when they've improved.'

'It's good practice.'

'This is what we've always done.'

'I can see where the gaps are.'

Naturally, she had more questions.

- What is it about these challenges that the pupils love?

- What values are being promoted around being right and looking smart?

- What is the impact on pupils' motivation if they don't improve quickly?

- How is this weekly data used to impact future outcomes? How often do you evaluate?

- Is this whole-school approach still fit for purpose? How do you know?

- Where are learners taking control of their own progress?

- Is this practice an effective use of pupils' and teachers' time?

'... but the children love them!'

In some cases, teachers just couldn't see how this process reinforced fixed mindset ideas: the 'clever' pupils scored highly and hence moved up, the 'not so clever' struggled and remained where they were until pupil progress meetings with senior leaders dictated an intervention. These somewhat predictable outcomes led to a decrease in effort and resilience from some pupils, particularly the 'clever' ones if they got something wrong. Ruchi distinctly remembers pupils turning their backs on their partners during this 'fun' challenge that they all 'loved so much'; the worry being that their work might be copied and lead to their partner getting a higher score. When teachers gave work back, it was examined in secret and hidden from peers because the children didn't want to share their score in case it exposed them as being bad at maths. Ruchi suspects that the children who 'loved it' were just confident enough to vocalise their relief at getting full marks. It created silent divisions in the classroom and, when asked about maths in general, pupils spoke about learning with a fixed vocabulary, commenting on who was good at maths and who needed more help. The children who loved maths were those who flourished. It broke Ruchi's heart, but strengthened her resolve to do better.

In this particular case, the teachers had lost their focus and needed to re-evaluate the forms and functions of assessment, with careful attention paid to *why* we use assessment in the classroom, *how* we can use it effectively and *who* it is for. With this in mind, better-informed decisions can be made about how to measure progress and attainment.

# SUMMATIVE VS FORMATIVE ASSESSMENT

Before we get stuck in, here's a quick recap of the features and functions of the different types of assessment:

| Summative assessment | Formative assessment |
| --- | --- |
| Done at the end of a unit, year, topic, phase, etc. to give a 'final' picture of what the children have learnt or know. Focus is on the outcome and on proving and measuring the learning. It's done to the learners and is externally referenced.<br><br>Examples include:<br>• Tests.<br>• Quizzes. | Done each lesson, throughout units of work, to give us knowledge about what the child knows at any given point. It informs our planning and our next steps to take with the children's learning. The focus is on the process of learning and on improvement. It's done with the learners and is personal.<br><br>Examples include:<br>• Marking and feedback in books. |

- Marking off objectives at the end of a unit.
- Key Stage 1 and Key Stage 2 SATs.
- Completing a 'What We Now Know' grid at the end of a topic.
- End of unit assessments.
- Spelling tests.
- Times tables tests.
- Key Stage 1 phonics check.

- Questioning in class.
- Supporting the children when you move around the class during independent work.
- Looking at the work they produce and tailoring the next activity to fit the understanding that the child has shown.
- Deploying AfL techniques in your interactions with children during lessons (e.g. targeting questions to certain children).

We want you to try out a little exercise. On a piece of paper, jot down all the ways in which your pupils are assessed in your classroom. Now think about how pupils are assessed across the school. What have you come up with? Can you group your answers? How many would you class as summative and how many as formative? Which assessment methods inform and impact learning within a lesson? A unit? A term? A year? Which ones don't have any impact? Can you get rid of any? Keep this piece of paper, it might come in handy later.

Assessment can be viewed as the collection and evaluation of materials that evidence learning. In other words, when we teach, we craft questions to elicit thinking in order for learning to take place. Instead of simply hoping, crossing our fingers and assuming that it's happened, we use assessments to either evidence proficiency or diagnose what needs work. On the surface, the link between assessment and mindset might not be clear, but let's think about it a little further. If assessments are broadly used to report successes or failures, they send powerful messages to pupils about learning. Think of those pupils who bypass written feedback and instead go straight to their score, the number of ticks, or how much red or green – depending on your marking policy – they have in their books. Who gets hung up on how many incorrect answers they have or has a deterministic view of how they might perform under pressure? These are your fixed-mindset pupils and these misconceptions about the relationship between assessment and learning can also shape their parents' beliefs. This was a bigger issue in the days of levels, when parents (and pupils) would get so fixated that the level became the focus of nearly all discussions about learning. We know that the number isn't really about *learning*, it simply represents a summative judgement on how successful (or worse, how unsuccessful) a pupil has been in that instance. The EEF noted:

> Awarding grades for every piece of work may reduce the impact of marking, particularly if pupils become preoccupied with grades at the expense of consideration of teachers' formative comments.[1]

Huntington School in York was part of a case study which suggested that feedback is more meaningful to the children when it is not accompanied by a summative judgement:

> Without a level to hang the comment on, teachers have been encouraged to think more deeply about what the feedback needs to say and do.[2]

Quality feedback can dig deeper into what the child has (or hasn't) done in a piece of work, moving them on far more effectively than giving them a mark out of 10 or a grade would. Julia clearly remembers being graded for a piece of religious education (RE) work at school: a picture showing an example of where we place our trust in something. Even at ten years old, she remembers thinking, 'How did the teacher make that decision? What's it based on?' She got an 8 out of 10, by the way. No ideas about how to improve, but she still remembers that she *was an 8* in RE back in 1991. This is another reason why the removal of levels was so necessary in primary education. We need to think carefully about what types of assessment will enable confidence, self-esteem and feelings of 'I *can* do this, I *can* improve.'

Research tells us that the intentional use of formative assessment to promote learning improves pupils' outcomes.[3] As we respond to our assessments, those formative strategies become fundamental tools to help us shape and adapt learning tasks. Teachers who use assessment as part of the learning process – rather than as a means to an end – can enhance pupil motivation, engagement, self-esteem and, when used within a meaningful learning framework, increase the active involvement of pupils in their own

---

1   Victoria Elliot, Jo-Anne Baird, Therese N. Hopfenbeck, Jenni Ingram, Ian Thompson, Natalie Usher, Mae Zantout, James Richardson and Robbie Coleman, *A Marked Improvement? A Review of the Evidence on Written Marking* (London: Education Endowment Foundation, 2016), p. 5.
2   Elliot et al., *A Marked Improvement?*, p. 32.
3   Dylan Wiliam and Paul Black, *Inside the Black Box: Raising Standards Through Classroom Assessment* (London: GL Assessment Ltd., 1990).

learning. You've got it, we're talking about our old friend metacognition again. If pupils are fixed in their view of assessment – by which we mean they understand assessment as providing information about success or failure, and attach value to this system – it's only going to lead to demotivation.

Day-to-day, your ongoing formative assessment helps you to challenge or support in order to maximise outcomes. When pupils are encouraged to review their own learning and apply these insights in future, they start to understand that they are in control of their outcomes, that they are able to improve by using the strategies, tools and practices they learn in the classroom. They learn through feedback, self-assessment, self-monitoring and critical evaluation and can make changes accordingly – what a wonderful way to connect feelings of ownership, confidence and independence to something as fear-inducing as assessment. All this reflection and growth leads to what we keep revisiting: lifelong learning behaviours.

The education system places a certain level of importance on summative assessments, which there is no escaping. Whatever you may think of SATs, let's agree to not let that distract us. Assessments *of* learning have a place in schools, and we don't think that's going to change anytime soon. The goal is not to fight against the system but to work with it and to use statutory testing to enhance our practice. We have to get savvy and move away from assessing one form of output. For example, how often do we assess English, science, geography, history, RE, PSHE, etc. based on a written outcome? Surely this isn't the only way for pupils to demonstrate their understanding. While we're on the topic, we have a gripe with *completed* work being the end goal. Is completed work a sign of completed learning? We're willing to bet you've taught pupils who rush to finish a task just so they can move onto the next one. You just know those fixed mindsets attach feelings of achievement to how much writing is on the page. But as we know, deep learning does have a place for 'I'm finished!' Are your pupils questioning, proving, creating and reflecting? If not, let's create assessment opportunities so pupils can demonstrate this. It's time to get creative.

# ASSESSMENT *OF, FOR* AND *AS* LEARNING

Assessment is cyclical in nature: we assess; use our findings to inform planning; teach or revisit content; and start again. The key is to understand how to move from assessment *of* learning to assessment *for* learning, then assessment *as* learning. Assessment is a powerful tool when we learn how to apply it using a principled approach.

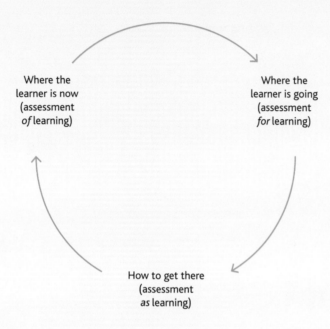

Where the learner is now (assessment *of* learning)

Where the learner is going (assessment *for* learning)

How to get there (assessment *as* learning)

Let's look a little closer at these three approaches.

Summative in nature and linked to fixed mindsets, assessment *of* learning:

- Usually takes place at the end of a unit or task to measure and evidence achievement.

- Can be used at the beginning of a unit to diagnose strengths and gaps in learning.

- Uses processes that make it possible for pupils to demonstrate their competence and skill.

- Is used as a basis to make judgements around attainment, and sometimes ability.

- Offers a range of alternative mechanisms for assessing the same outcomes.

Teacher-led, supportive and growth-promoting, assessment *for* learning:

- Occurs throughout the learning process.

- Involves teachers identifying the particular learning needs of different pupils or groups.

- Means selecting and adapting materials and resources.

- Has clear learning objectives.

- Means that pupils understand what successful work looks like and what the expectations are through modelling.

- Outlines clear success criteria, and it's even better if this is co-constructed with the learners.

- Uses differentiated questioning to assess what the children already know and to personalise feedback.

- Uses quality higher-order questions and question stems.

- Delivers regular and timely feedback from the teacher so pupils know how to improve.

- Systematically checks in with individuals, groups and the whole class to see how the learning is going.

- Involves dialogic teaching. Pupils and teachers engage in dialogue together.

- Involves a number of pupils in answering a single question, creating the opportunity for discussion and justifying answers with clear reasoning.

- Creates differentiated teaching strategies and learning opportunities to help individual pupils move forward in their learning.

- Encourages pupils to consult in their group or with a partner in order to formulate an answer.

- Shares the overall journey and outcomes with pupils to provide a clear purpose to learning.

- Shares success criteria with pupils, so they are able to identify where they were, where they are now and where they need to go next.

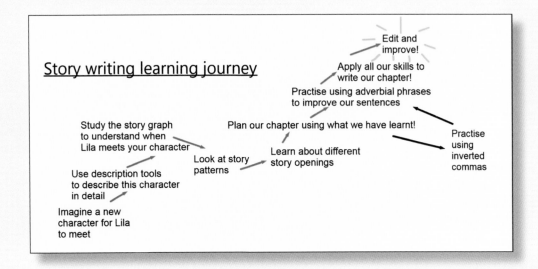

Assessment *as* learning emphasises assessment as a pupil-led process of metacognition:

- Through visible success criteria, pupils are able to identify where they were, where they are now and where they need to go next.

- Pupils are engaged in creating their own learning.

- Pupils reflect on their learning and actively seek feedback to improve.

- Pupils are encouraged to make sense of new information by relating it to prior knowledge.

- Pupils use the language of learning to analyse, compare and reflect on their work.

- Pupils use tools around them to independently self-assess and correct.

- Pupils understand that learning is an ongoing journey.

- Pupils collaborate to draw on each other's strengths and make progress.

- Pupils use high-quality models to peer- and self-assess, thus understanding what success looks like and if they've achieved it.

At the beginning of this chapter we talked about the function of assessment. Have a look at the list you made. What do you think of it now? What *is* the purpose of assessment? When you can answer this question confidently, you can start to make appropriate planning decisions about when to use assessment and what this assessment will look like.

## Getting the temperature right

We've talked about climate and culture a lot, and we think you have probably gathered how important it is to get this right in order to embed all the other principles we've talked about. Assessment is no different. Your pupils should punch the air when they know they will be given opportunities to self-reflect and improve; this should be associated with progress and they should understand what they can do to be even better. Wouldn't we expect this as professionals? So often we speak to teachers who feel disengaged when they have been observed and haven't received any feedback or, even worse, they've been appeased with woolly praise without any targets. Our pupils are no different, they need to *see* and, even better, *understand* that there is more they can do and further they can go. Assessment can make that visible to them.

The goal is to embed assessment *as* learning into the culture of your classroom. If you want your pupils to care, they've got to be part of the process; in fact, more than that, they've got to be active participants in the learning *and* assessment process.

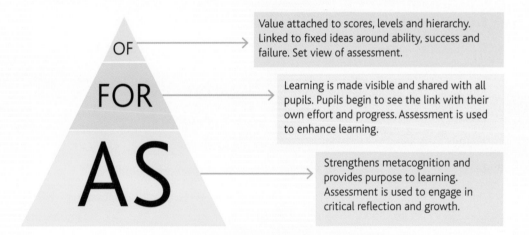

172

Post-levels, individual schools have become more autonomous in their marking and assessment policies, and assessment now lies in the hands of each school (apart from SATs and other statutory testing, of course). Therefore, schools are working far more collaboratively to develop their approaches. Moderation between classes, year groups and clusters of schools is now the norm – we all need to compare and contrast to secure our own judgements about whether work is of the expected standard, and what the standards should look like. Education is making big leaps with regard to summative assessments; it's not all doom and gloom, test scores and tracking grids. Comparative judgements are fast becoming the go-to approach when assessing writing, and this relies on the teacher's professional expertise and judgements to make informed decisions about writing outcomes. Hooray! Let's have more of this, please! Professional integrity needs more good press – so much has been written by teachers on blogs and social media about the 'accountability regime' driving bad practice around assessment, but change is definitely in the air. Summative assessments *do* have a role to play, so here's one last tip: just be wise with how you present this information to your pupils, parents and colleagues, as it's easy for the data to take over the personal successes of each individual and – before you know it – we have a cohort of numbers, colours, bands and letters, which is *not* going to produce lifelong learners.

## SOLO taxonomy, again

The solo model + assessment = assessment *as* learning

While we have already explored SOLO taxonomy in lots of detail, we want to reiterate how valuable and useful the model can be, not only for differentiation, but as a self-assessment tool. In fact, the model is gathering a lot of momentum in UK primary schools through the Learning First movement.[4] Mark our words, every school will be using it in some form before long and you could be one of those teachers who smugly says, 'Oh, it's nothing new, I was using it ages ago.' SOLO helps teachers to formulate and tweak their success criteria and learning objectives. It also allows for a culture of conversational feedback between peers, as well as between teacher and learners.

---

4   See https://learningfirst.com/.

# PLANNING

Although we're fairly confident that most teachers use formative strategies every day in their regular practice, the moment you grab assessment by the horns and consciously use it to make informed decisions about next steps is when it will start to demonstrably impact on pupil outcomes. You need to develop your own metacognition around pedagogy before your pupils can develop theirs. Our tip would be to start thinking overtly about assessment in your regular planning. Instead of thinking about a plenary, think about building in assessment opportunities throughout the lesson.

In the planning example that follows, consider how many opportunities there are for discussion between the teacher and the children. In all the active learning, in which the children are using manipulatives or discussing ideas, there are opportunities for talking about what they know. There are times for paired work. There are key questions which signpost the learning to the children. With your burgeoning knowledge of Bloom's, can you see where on the hierarchy these activities and questions lie? What are the children being encouraged to see, do, think about and learn? Pre-empting common misconceptions will also guide the teacher in the metacognitive conversations that are necessary to deepen everyone's understanding. When we plan for this, it happens. Only rarely can a teacher remember all they wanted to provide in a lesson when it's in full flow. Think ahead for the clearest path.

**Learning objective (LO):** To round any whole number – e.g. 437, 437,000, 437,073, 4,370,073.

To use different contexts verbally – e.g. £, g, km.

| Key vocabulary | | Learning resources/manipulatives | Outcomes for the week/learning journey |
|---|---|---|---|
| Whole hundred thousand | Between | Base 10 (dienes blocks) so pupils can build the numbers to decide what it's closest to. | Re-visit and practise place value up to six digits. |
| Whole ten thousand | Rounded | Counters. | Rounding numbers up to six digits. |
| Million | Place value | Place value charts (A4 laminated). | Secure understanding of what zero represents. |
| | | | Rounding to 2, 3, 4, 5 and 6 places (build up). |

| Identified pupils working below age-related expectations:<br>JB, CB, TR, EF, GS (initials of children) | Identified pupils working above age-related expectations:<br>RO, PA, FS, TT, IW (initials of children) | Pupils from vulnerable groups (English as an additional language/pupil premium):<br>JB, CB, TT, TR, LS (initials of children) | **Special educational needs and disabilities (SEND)/behaviour support to be provided by teacher** |
|---|---|---|---|

| Main learning | Points of difficulty | Independent tasks | Greater depth | Support | Assessment opportunities |
|---|---|---|---|---|---|
| Rounding up to six-digit numbers to the nearest ten, ten thousand and hundred thousand. Ping-pong lesson starter – place value chart and counters. Pupils make the numbers with counters.<br><br>**Key questions:**<br>What are the 'rules' we use when rounding? Which place value chart column do we need to look at when we round to the nearest hundred thousand? When is it best to round to one thousand? When is it best to round to ten thousand? Can you justify your reasoning? | Recognising and saying five- or six-digit numbers.<br><br>Practise this first using repetition. Choose numbers that will challenge place value – e.g. 437,073.<br><br>Confusing the nearest thousand and nearest ten thousand. Practise this orally. Pre-teaching in assembly for pupils working below age-related expectations. | (The aim is to provide a cumulative degree of challenge.)<br><br>Write out one hundred and thirty-seven thousand, five hundred and seventy-two as a number. Increase the number by 2,000.<br><br>347 is between _00 and _00.<br><br>347 is between 340 and ____.<br><br>347 rounded to the nearest 100 is ____.<br><br>347 rounded to the nearest 10 is ____. | Ed says: My number is 1,350 when rounded to the nearest ten.<br><br>Joe says: Mine is 1,400 when rounded to the nearest hundred.<br><br>Both numbers are whole numbers.<br><br>What is the greatest possible difference between the two numbers?<br><br>The greatest possible difference is 104 because 1,449 – 1,345 = 104. | Teacher to play place value game first, matching spoken words to written words, pictorial representation and number.<br><br>What is the value of each digit? What is the value of ____ in this number? (Pictorial representation.)<br><br>Place value charts for game with LS and CB. Round numbers to nearest ten. | Whiteboards to assess during starter and number talk. Use this to identify key groups.<br><br>Independent task to assess understanding.<br><br>Whiteboards to assess during starter and number talk. Use this to identify key groups. |

| | | | | |
|---|---|---|---|---|
| **Sentence stems:**<br><br>___ is the exact number.<br><br>___ rounded to the nearest whole thousand is ___.<br><br>I know this because ...<br><br>___ is between ___ and ___.<br><br>It is closest to ___.<br><br>**Number talk:**<br><br>Robert says 437,697 rounded to the nearest 10,000 is 440,697. Is he right? Talk and prove. | Oral practice and rehearsal of recognising place value.<br><br>Kiera rounded 2,215,678 to the nearest million and wrote 2,215,000. Can you explain to Kiera what mistake she has made and why she has done it?<br><br>Create a toolkit to help others round numbers successfully (success criteria). | Pupils to explain their reasoning then write their own story with different numbers. Swap with another child and discuss.<br><br>Pair up children: RO, PA, TT, IW.<br><br>FS to work independently. | Show answer when rounding to nearest hundred and thousand. What do you notice? (Hint: zeros.)<br><br>Can you predict what it will be when rounding to the nearest ten thousand? | Independent task to assess understanding. |

**Key**

| Where might the learning slow down?<br><br>What misconceptions will you plan for?<br><br>Where will pupils get stuck and how will they overcome this? | What will the children be doing to consolidate their learning and challenge themselves?<br><br>How is this differentiated so that every child is challenged and achieves the LO? | A problem/task that relies on applying the new learning, taking it a stage further. Which scaffolds will be removed? | What immediate intervention is used to support all children to achieve? | How will you/the pupils assess understanding and progress?<br><br>E.g. peer- and self-assessment, verbal feedback, guided groups, mini-assessment task, AfL, reflective learning log, etc. |
|---|---|---|---|---|

Planning scaffold examples

# AFL FINAL THOUGHTS

- Give clear, concise learning objectives. Every child should be able to articulate what they are learning in the lesson.

- Make everything visible and clear. Pupils should understand the learning process and where they are in that journey.

- Give children a chance to have a go *before* teacher input and instruction – use this to assess understanding.

- Co-construct clear success criteria.

- Use whiteboards or a visualiser to 'check in' throughout the lesson and model successes and mistakes – think mini-plenaries.

- Practise differentiated questioning. Try Pose-Pause-Pounce-Bounce. This formula for asking a question was created by Pam Fearnley.[5] It involves posing the question to the class; pausing to wait for everyone to formulate a response; asking a targeted child for an answer; bouncing that answer to another child to ask what they thought of it, or what we can build onto the first child's answer.

- Use children's work to pose questions and give feedback.

- Replace hands up with talk partners. You could try Frank Lyman's Think, Pair, Share: think about it on your own; discuss it with your talk partner; get ready to share your answer with the rest of the class.[6]

- Dialogic teaching.

- Regular self- and peer-assessment.

---

5   Pose-Pause-Pounce-Bounce is a concept created by Pam Fearnley of Pupils First (UK) Ltd and is now taught in schools across the UK. pamb566@btinternet.com.

6   Frank Lyman, The Responsive Classroom Discussion: The Inclusion of All Students. In Audrey Anderson (ed.), *Mainstreaming Digest* (College Park, MD: University of Maryland Press, 1981), pp. 109–113.

- Include lots of modelling, success criteria, shared talk and examples at the beginning, then slowly take away the scaffolds. Encourage pupils to 'go deeper' and get 'stuck'.

- Work with different groups of children so that you can check in with everyone at least once.

- Compare with your assessment from the beginning of the lesson to measure progress.

Chapter 10

# LESSON IDEAS

While it's all very well to understand the theory behind growth mindset, what really matters is making it part and parcel of your children's school experience, so that it becomes second nature. Our whole purpose as teachers is to tailor classroom activities to the children, so we've put together a bank of workable lesson ideas from which you can pick and choose. They range from activities to try with nursery children, all the way through to activities to prepare your Year 6s for their leap into secondary school.

There are 39 lessons so that if you wanted, you could use one every week of your school year. Many of them are adaptable to specific curriculum areas and could therefore serve as lesson starters or plenaries. Feel free to adapt as necessary to make each lesson work for you and your pupils. The only goal is to embed these kinds of activities so that the children develop a growth mindset organically, day by day. The lesson ideas are, of course, supported by the culture, environment and language that you already have in place.

Let's avoid lessons and activities that rely on the word 'yet'; growth mindset is so much more than that. These lessons are about becoming comfortable with the features of growth mindset, which go much deeper than language. It's developing the characteristics of a person with a growth mindset rather than a fixed one. What an impact we'll have if we develop 30 children's characteristics at once. Trickle that through, year by year, and you'll soon end up with a school whose children are motivated by their own effort, and where pupils are instrumental in achieving their own learning goals. These lessons act as more than stand-alone sessions that operate in isolation. As you've no doubt realised, they'll act as a springboard into discussion. Your role as a teacher is to encourage the children to make links between their own mindset and the skills they're developing, and how this will contribute to their overall success as lifelong learners.

With that in mind, we've classified the lesson ideas using symbols to help you judge which will be spot-on for your class. We truly believe that they will be valuable for all children aged 3–11, but to help you, they are coded by age-appropriateness.

**Lesson focus**

| Resilience | Challenge | Higher-order thinking | Effort | Collaboration | Explicit growth mindset teaching |
|---|---|---|---|---|---|
|  |  |  |  |  (collaboration) |  |

**Suitable for**

| Whole class | Group work | Pair work |
|---|---|---|
|  |  |  |

**Amount of time needed**

| Short (15 minutes) | Medium (30 minutes) | Long (1 hour) | Half a day or more |
|---|---|---|---|
|  |  |  |  |

**Designed for**

| EYFS | Key Stage 1 | Key Stage 2 | All |
|---|---|---|---|
|  |  |  |  |

## Baby Predictions

### Intention(s)

To encourage the children to realise that making mistakes leads to learning and, ultimately, more success.

### Resources

Pictures and video clips of babies at different stages of learning to walk.

Scarves or other ties for the three-legged walking task.

### Activity

Display three pictures on the board:

1. A 0–5-month-old baby.
2. A baby who has fallen over while trying to walk.
3. An older baby, sitting.

Ask the children to predict which baby will learn to walk first, and to justify their thinking. Do they think it'll be the older baby? Do they think the baby who has fallen over is less likely to walk than the others? Why?

Show short video clips of babies learning to walk, and falling over in their attempts, to increase discussion and elicit ideas from the children. If the children have younger siblings, perhaps they could be invited in to show your class how trying and failing leads to learning the skill.

Lead the discussion to the fact that if a baby just sits, and doesn't try to walk, there is no possibility of learning to do so. If a baby keeps on falling over, it is working out what it needs to do in order to become stable on its feet. The only way it can learn how to walk successfully is by trying repeatedly.

Allow the children to try the skill out for themselves by having a three-legged walkabout. The children are unlikely to master it on the first attempt, but as they stumble and fall, they learn how to make themselves stable and achieve success.

Elouise (Year 1) said: 'The big baby is the strongest but then we saw him just sit there! When we try it's called practising.'

## Blind Buddy

Challenge    collaboration

### Intention(s)

To help the children to become comfortable with feeling unsure. Reinforce the idea that success or failure often doesn't even come into a task, and that collaboration helps us to improve.

### Resources

Something to act as a blindfold (one per pair).

Paper and pencils.

### Activity

In pairs, the children decide who will be the artist, and who will be the guide. The guide is going to decide what the artist will draw. For younger children, this could be something in the classroom, or it could be something more abstract and imaginative for older pupils. In any case, the artist will be blindfolded during the activity.

The guide helps the artist to draw the identified object/scene/thing by describing what they need to do. The guide should give all the instructions, from how to use the materials, to where the marks need to go on the paper. The guide may only use words – they shouldn't direct the artist's hand to help.

At regular intervals, ask the artists how they are feeling. Are they excited? Nervous about what they have actually managed to draw? Do they feel helpless? Are they enjoying the task, without thinking about how 'good' their finished creation will be? Ask the guides too. Their feelings might be similar. Do they feel responsible for the success of the picture? Discuss the merits (or negatives) of some of these feelings.

When the children mutually decide that they have finished the picture, ask the artists to predict what they will see when they remove the blindfold. Ask the guides to describe the picture to the artist. What is their reaction? The children can then look at the art together. Is it as they expected?

If you have time, after the paired discussion, it would be lovely to let them draw the object again, this time with them both

Paint (if desired, and you are feeling brave!).

Card (optional extension).

as artists; both using their sight. They will be in a collaborative frame of mind and will value each other's input.

In Key Stage 2 you could adapt this lesson so that the children are drawing for themselves and tracking their own improvement. In this lesson, the 'blind buddy' is the tool they will use to draw with.

Pre-prepare small pieces of card (roughly A6 size – enough to cover a hand) with a pencil-sized hole in the middle. The children will need to push their pencil through and hold it underneath, so that the card is covering their drawing hand. When they come to draw, they shouldn't be able to see what they are doing.

You can provide a simple object to draw (a sharpener, pen, scissors, etc.) or they can attempt to draw their other hand if they'd prefer a challenge. The children will find it strange at first and worry about drawing it 'right'; however, when they try to improve their drawing each time they should be able to track their progress and comment on specific things that have improved. Have a break in the middle of the session and use a visualiser to model progress. Present the attempts out of sequence and invite peers to suggest which was the first drawing, which was the last and why.

Emily (Year 3) said: 'I felt nervous when I was drawing because I didn't want it to be rubbish. But then I started to relax and just enjoyed it because it was funny.'

Tyler (Year 3) said: 'I trust Megan so we did it as a team. She was a good guide because she used good words to help me know where to put my lines.'

## A Tall Task

| Intention(s) | Activity |
|---|---|
| To help the children learn that just because they cannot accomplish something on their own, it isn't failing. | Place a large pile of books on one side of the classroom. There should be far more than one child could carry – so many that they won't even attempt to. Select a volunteer and ask them to carry the pile of books to the other side of the classroom. |

**Intention(s)**

To help the children learn that just because they cannot accomplish something on their own, it isn't failing.

**Resources**

A pile of books.

**Activity**

Place a large pile of books on one side of the classroom. There should be far more than one child could carry – so many that they won't even attempt to. Select a volunteer and ask them to carry the pile of books to the other side of the classroom.

If the child is hesitant, discuss why as a class. Does it feel like too big a task to be achievable?

How could they successfully carry out the task? Support the children to make a plan. Among other ideas, they might decide to:

- Get a group of children to carry a couple of books each.
- Assign a role to each person in class (one picks a book up, one hands it to the next person, etc.).
- Make a chain of children to pass the books along like a conveyor belt.

Discuss the phrase 'many hands make light work'. Does this apply here? Is it a good phrase to live by all the time? Or should we sometimes rise to a tricky challenge independently?

Explain to the children that the pile of books is a metaphor for a tricky piece of work. Just because one child can't carry all the books in one go, it doesn't mean they have failed. Thinking of sensible ways to get help – like breaking it down into smaller chunks or seeking help from your peers – means that you can share ideas and expertise, and ultimately be successful at whatever has been asked of you.

Logan (Year 2) said: 'I think I could do it on my own because I'm strong, but if I let someone else help, it would be easier to move.'

## Gappy Wall

EFFORT

Explicit growth
mindset

### Intention(s)

To show the children that gaps make for a weaker structure. If we fill our brains with experiences and learning, then our brains become stronger, with more connections built for future learning.

### Resources

Approximately 20 building blocks per group of children.

Weights.

### Activity

Put the children in groups of three or four. Give each group a number of building blocks and ask them to make a wall. Tell them that the wall must be full of gaps.

When the children have built their walls, ask them to experiment with placing weights on top. How much weight does each wall support before it collapses?

Ask the children to consider why the wall isn't very stable. Explain how the gaps affect its stability and strength.

Now ask the groups to make a solid wall, ensuring that there are no gaps in its construction. Repeat the experiment by placing weights on top. Help the children to realise that the solid walls can support a much heavier load.

Draw the analogy between the walls and the children's brains. If we make our brains 'full' by completing work, taking part in activities and experiencing new things, we create more neural pathways and connections. In turn, this makes our brains stronger and more intelligent. A brain with more connections is a wall without gaps.

Emmy (Year 6) said: 'I like thinking of ways to fill the gaps in my brain. It's like when I read a book, I find out things I don't normally think of. That can be another building block for me.'

## A Pride of Puppets

Explicit growth mindset

### Intention(s)

To introduce the children to some key learning behaviours of growth mindset using puppets. The children see the traits at play and understand their value.

### Resources

Different puppets or toys to portray each growth mindset characteristic.

### Activity

Introduce the children to learning puppets. These puppets act out situations in which they show a characteristic of being a successful learner. They each show different learning skills that the children can emulate and develop in themselves. Examples of the puppets and skills could include:

- Christopher Caterpillar – concentration.
- Dominic Duck – don't give up, resilience.
- Tabitha Tortoise and Theodore Tortoise – be cooperative.
- Christian Camel – be curious.
- Hugh Hedgehog – have a go.
- Isaac Spider – use your imagination.
- Ivan Insect – keep improving, reflectiveness.
- Edward Elephant – enjoy learning.

Encourage the children to join in with storytelling by imaginary mini-plays or scenes in which the animal is showing their learning skill. Model this for the children first. You could leave the puppets out for the children to use during independent learning, and see what stories they create.

Whenever you are sharing a story in which a character shows one of these learning skills, refer to the puppets and use them to reinforce the idea with the children.

Jack (Year 1) said: 'I told my dad he was being like Ivan Insect yesterday because he used lots of different screwdrivers to fix our bath plug.'

## Super Story Time

Explicit growth mindset

### Intention(s)

For the children to engage with books on the topic of growth mindset and reinforce the traits and ideas that are presented in their environment.

### Resources

Books related to growth mindset.

### Activity

Story time is a gold-plated opportunity to convey the messages of growth mindset. Share a story and discuss the characters and messages that the children notice. Can they relate the story to an event or learning experience in their own life?

There is a list of suggested books to use in the references and further reading section. You could use these books for guided reading (in groups or as a whole class) to further explore the language of mindset. Unpick exactly which words demonstrate the key ideas of mindset, and how the author leads us to the inferences that they intend.

Jake (Year 4) said: 'When I write stories, I like characters who make things better by the end.'

## Rewrite History

RESILIENCE

Explicit growth mindset

### Intention(s)

For the children to explore a growth mindset story in more depth, imagining and discussing what might have happened if part of the story was changed.

### Resource

A growth mindset fiction book of your choice.

### Activity

Read a fiction story (see the references and further reading section for recommendations) and explore the plot thoroughly. Encourage the children to discuss how the characters were ultimately successful in showing growth mindset traits.

Ask the children to rewrite the story (or part of it) to explore what would have happened if their mindset had remained fixed. Sometimes it's valuable to see the traits from the other side to appreciate how a fixed mindset doesn't get as good results.

The children could then share their own stories. Are they all the same? Did the same types of events occur? Why? Why not?

William (Year 5) said: 'It was hard to change the ending as I already knew what actually happens. But I worked hard and in the end I liked my ending better. It's more interesting and helps people to know that nothing is ever too hard.'

## Neuron-Firing Non-Fiction

Explicit growth
mindset

### Intention(s)

To expose the children to quality non-fiction texts about the brain and how its biology and structure are interlinked with growth mindset.

### Resources

Non-fiction books about the brain, intelligence and IQ.

Small notebooks.

### Activity

Allow the children free access to a variety of non-fiction texts. Give them each a little 'Brain Notes' book, in which they can record interesting facts. They could illustrate the cover with drawings inspired by the non-fiction books. Whenever they discover something interesting about the brain (in lessons or from reading the books), they can jot it down. It'll become a journal of their expanding knowledge about the theory and anatomy of growth mindset.

You could house these books in a special basket or on a shelf in your reading area. Children adore general knowledge and something as magical as the brain will get them excited and fire their imagination about what is going on inside their own skulls, as well as firing their neurons!

Use extracts from the non-fiction books as guided reading, or create comprehension quizzes from them as a way to get growth mindset running through all areas of the classroom.

Kasper (Reception) said: 'Woah. How is that even possible?!'

## Inspirational Lives

| Intention(s) | Activity |
|---|---|
| For the children to be inspired by other people, and to understand that people can change their own lives and outcomes. | Introduce the children to a public figure or celebrity who has shown a growth mindset in their personal or professional life. Show them photos of important points in their life and do a mini biographical study. |
| | Write down a series of key life events on pieces of card – including those which show the features of a growth mindset – one event per card. Mix them up and give them to the children. Ask them to order the life event cards into the correct sequence. This will initiate a good discussion about how failure ultimately turns into success. |
| | Some good examples of people to study are: |
| | Steve Jobs |
| **Resources** | Michael Jordan |
| Photos and a child-accessible biography, tailored to the point you wish to make about mindset. | The Beatles |
| | Eminem |
| | Walt Disney |
| | Oprah Winfrey |
| | Albert Einstein |
| | Dame Ellen MacArthur |

Denisas (Year 4) said: 'I want to do something like that when I am an adult. It means there is a good reason for you doing that job.'

## What's it Worth?

Higher-order thinking

### Intention(s)

To encourage the children to adapt their view quickly, and learn to be flexible with their answers and understanding.

### Resources

Different-coloured counters.

### Activity

Present the children with some tiddlywink-sized counters in different colours. Announce that each colour is worth a certain value (adjust this to the children's level of mathematical understanding).

Pick out a selection of counters. How much are they worth?

Then change the values, or add and take away counters. How much are they worth now?

Keep moving the goalposts of what you expect from their answers or reasoning. It'll feel like mental gymnastics, and it's a quick game to revisit over and over again.

The more the children get used to the expectations changing (and having to deal with the ever-evolving reasoning that goes with it), the more they will welcome the unknown. This is training them to be flexible.

Polly (Year 1) said: 'It is fun to always be changing. It means I have to listen hard or I will miss what happens next!'

## Elastic Band Bonanza

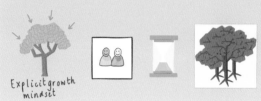

Explicit growth
mindset

### Intention(s)

To help the children to see the brain as a connected web of neurons, and to realise that the more connections we make, the deeper and richer our understanding will be.

### Resources

Geoboards and elastic bands.

### Activity

After the children have learnt some of the key facts about neuron pathways in the brain, allow them access to geoboards (these are boards studded with plastic pegs that you can hook rubber bands around to make shapes and patterns) and rubber bands.

Ask the children to put three rubber bands on the geoboard. Talk about how there are lots of gaps and how the bands don't really connect to anything.

Gradually increase the number of elastic bands you give to the children. Explain that as they increase the number of bands, this is just like how the web of neurons in the brain gets fuller and more connected. This shows how the brain can understand more and make more links when your neurons are firing and creating new pathways.

Explain the analogy to the children to ensure that they understand how our brains make links when we experience new challenges.

Valentina (Year 3) said: 'Is it possible to keep adding more and more? Does the brain ever get so full you can't add any more?'

## Mind the Gap!

Explicit growth mindset

### Intention(s)

To encourage the children to understand the complex web of connections in the brain and how we can build our intelligence by firing new connections.

### Resources

Diagrams of the London Underground system.

Poster paper and pens.

### Activity

Introduce the children to the London Tube map. What is it? Why are there so many lines? What would happen if there was only one line? Show them an individual line and demonstrate that if this was the only route, they could not make their way around the large city.

Explore the analogy between the web of underground lines and the web of neural pathways in their brains. The more we experience and learn, the more connections we make. Our intelligence gets stronger and our brains are more capable of helping us reach conclusions.

The children could then start to design their own neural tube map, labelling the stations as experiences or successes they've had. The lines connecting them show them how they got there.

Javan (Year 6) said: 'When you have to plan a journey, you can use the map. I'm going to use mine like a diary to remind myself of what I've done.'

## Living Links

Explicit growth mindset

| Intention(s) | Activity |
|---|---|
| To help the children see explicit links they've made between experiences in their own lives. | After a school event or trip, ask the children to relate aspects of it to other life experiences. Draw a simple spider diagram on a piece of poster paper and write the name of the event or trip in the middle. Ask the children to make a link between the trip and something from their own life experience and add it to the web. If appropriate, the children could draw their own representations onto the web.

You'll end up with a colourful group web, showing links and pathways – just like the pathways in the brain. You could even keep it on display and let the children add more ideas as they occur to them. |

**Resources**

An experience to act as a prompt.

Poster paper and pens.

Jack (nursery) said: 'I like the ducks at the farm. Nanny feeds the ducks at her pond.'

## Real-Life Hero

RESILIENCE  Challenge  EFFORT  collaboration

### Intention(s)

To show the children growth mindset at work in a real-life, relatable person.

### Resource

A suitable and willing candidate!

### Activity

Have a think about anyone in your local community who could come in to talk to your class about something they have done which meant they overcame the odds. Some ideas might be:

- A female professional who has made it in a male-dominated occupation.
- Someone who has succeeded in a certain role despite a known barrier, such as dyslexia.
- Someone who has overcome a phobia or fear.
- Someone who has encouraged others to achieve something extraordinary.
- A local sporting hero who has worked incessantly to gain their success.

The children could prepare questions in advance, and then write up an account of the visit, describing the effect that person has had on their mindset.

Rosy (Year 5) said: 'I liked it when she said her friend told her to try getting a different job, and she said she'd never want to do anything else. She proved her friend wrong in the end, didn't she?!'

## A Box of Mistakes

RESILIENCE

Explicit growth mindset

| Intention(s) | Activity |
|---|---|
| To encourage the children to become comfortable with making mistakes, and to recognise how to learn from them. | Bring in a special and beautiful box. A shoebox covered in lovely wrapping paper will do just fine. Name it 'The Box of Mistakes'. |
| | Ask each child to write down a mistake they have made in recent weeks or months on a piece of paper, and place the paper in the box. During circle time, pull some examples out of the box and discuss how that person could learn from the mistake and use it to better themselves. |
| | Ask the children if that person would like to admit to the mistake, so you can celebrate the growth and reflect on whether they did indeed change as a result of the mistake. |
| **Resources** | In a safe and challenging classroom, where growth mindset is being encouraged to flourish, children can be wonderfully forthcoming. |
| Paper, a box and honest children. | |

Lauren (Year 2) said: 'If we know that these are mistakes, why do we do them in the first place?'

## Maths Eyes

Higher-order thinking

### Intention(s)

To engage the children in evolving discussion, help them learn from others' ideas and to encourage them to make cross-curricular links to growth mindset.

### Resources

Suitable photos of everyday scenes in which maths can be discovered in abundance.

### Activity

Find images that are rich in 'hidden maths', like the example that follows. Ask the children the simple question, 'What maths can you see?' Annotate the picture to show all the different ideas the children come up with.

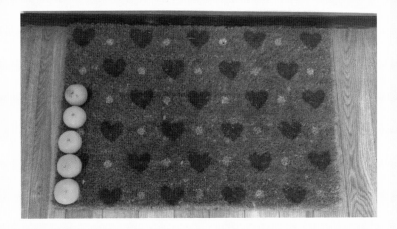

For this example, the children might offer:

'I think it would take eight oranges to complete the left-hand side. If the left-hand side is eight oranges tall, then the right-hand side would be too, because it's a rectangle.'

'I can see three rows of five hearts, and three rows of four hearts. 3 x 5 = 15. 3 x 4 = 12. So the total number of hearts = 15 + 12 = 27.'

Asking this open-ended question encourages the wonderful higher-order thinking that we want the children to become comfortable with. The more they practise their reasoning, the more connected their maths learning will become.

Callum (Year 6) said: 'When we do this, I think of the last thing we've done in maths, and there's normally something in the picture that relates to it. If not, I go for a calculation that fits, because there is always something you can calculate in a picture.'

## See it, Feel it, Show it

Explicit growth mindset

| Intention(s) | Activity |
| --- | --- |
| To arm the children with the emotional intelligence to talk about the feelings involved in mindset. | Teach the children about – or refresh their memory of – growth mindset traits:<br>• resilience<br>• challenge<br>• higher-order thinking<br>• effort<br>• collaboration |
| **Resources**<br>Modelling putty and art materials. | Have a class discussion about the feelings involved in each of these learning behaviours. What does it feel like in the body? What does it look like on the face? Can the children decide which colours match the feelings? Can they draw what they feel like? Make them with the modelling putty – is the feeling you get spiky or smooth? |

The more we can describe how we feel in situations when the traits are being tested, the more able we are to deal with the emotional aspects of growth mindset.

Gustas (nursery) said: 'My mummy is red when she is working in the garden.'

## Brain Hats

Explicit growth mindset

### Intention(s)

To teach the children about the anatomy and functions of the brain.

### Resources

Models and pictures as appropriate.

Brain hat template.

### Activity

Show the children a range of diagrams, models or pictures of the brain. Discuss how the brain has different sections, and name them if appropriate. Explain that the brain's different sections have different purposes.

Design a template that the children can cut out and construct to make their own brain hat.[1] They can put these on as an aid to help them understand the anatomy of the brain.

During a PE lesson Megan (Year 3) pointed to Julia's motor cortex and said: 'Mrs Stead, you're using that part of your brain because you're moving in a tricky way with Harry.'

---

1   Our favourite template can be found online at: http://ellenjmchenry.com/homeschool-freedownloads/lifesciences-games/documents/BrainHatColor.pdf.

## Brain Elasticity

Explicit growth
mindset

| Intention(s) | Activity |
|---|---|
| To understand that the brain is malleable, and that intelligence can be improved. To introduce the children to neuroplasticity. | Find a recipe to make slime.[2] Make some as a class, describing and discussing the properties of the material, including the elasticity.<br><br>Explain to the children that the slime is like the brain. It can be:<br>• stretched<br>• moulded<br>• reshaped |
| **Resources**<br><br>Ingredients to make slime. | Discuss the analogy and link this to the ways in which we can expand the brain – adding more information, seeking challenges that create new pathways and making sure we never stay static in our learning. |

Jamie (Year 1) said: 'I like feeling the change in my fingers. It changes like our bodies can change.'

---

2   Recipes abound on the internet, we like this one: https://theimaginationtree.com/easy-uk-slime-recipe-contact-lens-solution/.

## Function Fun

Explicit growth
mindset

### Intention(s)

To understand
the functions
of the brain.

### Resources

Cards
depicting
areas of
the brain
and brain
functions.

### Activity

Play a matching pairs game, which links the areas of the brain
and their different functions. Arrange all the cards face down
and ask the children to take it in turns to match the pairs.
Discuss the information as they turn the cards over.

Here are suggestions for the content of the cards:

| | | |
|---|---|---|
| Frontal lobe | Behaviour, our personality, planning and problem-solving | Motor cortex |
| Making our body move | Sensory cortex | Interpreting sensations from the body |
| Parietal lobe | Mental maths, spelling, making sense of things | Occipital lobe |
| Vision | Temporal lobe | Memory, language |

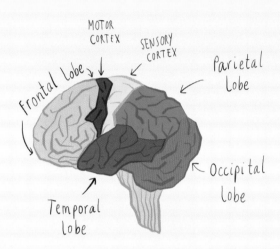

Rio (Year 4) said: 'We probably use our frontal lobe during every lesson.'

## Plenary Ponderings

Higher-order thinking

| Intention(s) | Activity |
|---|---|
| To introduce questioning to develop thinking skills. | Bob Eberle suggested some great ways of introducing growth mindset into plenaries.[3] Just a few clever questions a day can have long-lasting effects in your classroom. He developed the acronym SCAMPER to encourage creative thinking:<br><br>• **Substitute** – what other word or idea could we use instead? |

3   Bob Eberle, *Scamper: Games for Imagination Development* (Waco, TX: Prufrock Press, 2008).

Resources

None.

- **Combine** – how could these two ideas/numbers/words go together?

- **Adapt for a purpose** – how could you use this thing/idea/skill/approach for something else? What could that other use be?

- **Modify** – how could we change this to be more accurate/effective/appealing?

- **Purpose** – what else could we use this knowledge for?

- **Eliminate** – would it still make sense if we took something away? What could we remove?

- **Rearrange or reverse** – what would happen if we turned this calculation around? What could we make from this if we swap things around or mix them up?

A nice idea would be to display a bank of reminders next to the whiteboard. This would be a good aide memoire for you to ask spontaneous questions. As you read a story, for example, explore the SCAMPER questions. This doesn't have to be done rigidly or form a separate routine – they can be applied to all sorts of learning experiences.

Caleb (Year 5) said: 'I like it when we change things around because it means we have to think in an opposite way to what we normally think like.'

## A Mystery to Solve

Higher-order
thinking

### Intention(s)

To encourage
the children
to think in a
different way,
so that when
they face
something
they haven't
seen before,
or need
to think
differently,
they aren't
overstretched.

### Resources

Everyday
or unusual
objects or
pictures of
them.

### Activity

In a similar vein to Plenary Ponderings, our aim is to encourage creative thinking, and to reinforce the idea that things are never fixed. Presenting children with a task in which they have to question and change things means that they become comfortable with change and elastic thinking. We're focusing on creating the right classroom environment and conditions for thinking.

Show the children an everyday object – for example, a tap, a piece of string or a remote control. Ask:

- What else could this be?

- How many different uses for the item can you think of?

- What would happen if …? (For example, your item stopped working while you were using it?)

You could extend this by showing them an unusual item – for example, a rusty key, a bolt, a map, a nugget of silver or a strange-looking utensil – and asking, 'What could this be for?'

Or try making up words – for example, hablot, squeddle, pravick, mibula. Ask:

- What is this word?

- Can you draw it?

- Can you write a sentence with it in?

- Can you describe what it means?

These kinds of activities needn't take up many minutes in a day. You could use them as a little starter each morning while you do the register. Even – or perhaps especially – the youngest children would enjoy it, and the responses you get are likely to be priceless.

Alfie (Reception) said: 'A tap could pour out whatever you want. I would like it to be a tap for hot chocolate.'

## It's Not So Scary!

RESILIENCE    Challenge

| Intention(s) | Activity |
|---|---|
| To encourage the children to face a challenge with confidence. | Read *Shark in the Park* by Nick Sharratt.[4] Discuss how the pictures make it look like a scary shark is lurking, but how there isn't actually anything to be afraid of in the park. Make the link between this and how challenges often feel a little scary. However, once you look at the challenge with a growth mindset, you realise that you can overcome it and that things usually aren't as hard as you initially think. |
| **Resources**<br><br>A copy of *Shark in the Park* by Nick Sharratt.<br><br>Art materials and paper. | Make a class book of things that look or feel scary at first, but turn out to be positive. You could use lift-the-flap devices, or cut out a hole in the paper similar to the stimulus book *Shark in the Park*.<br><br>Share this with another class and talk about the feelings that all the children had when exploring the book. |

Ava (nursery) said: 'He's silly because he still thinks it's a shark!'

---

4   Nick Sharratt, *Shark in the Park* (London: Corgi Picture Books, 2000).

## Move the Goalposts

Higher-order thinking

| Intention(s) | Activity |
|---|---|
| To show the children that feeling on edge in their learning is part of a positive challenge. | Set the children off on a task and then change the expectations several times during the activity. This can lead to hilarity and wonderful creativity from the children. The task is almost irrelevant here – it's the process of making the children feel at ease with being on edge during their learning that is important. These kinds of experiences help to make the classroom ethos one of flexibility and positivity towards change. Move the goalposts multiple times to encourage resilience. |

An example might be:

**Resources**

General classroom resources.

Introduce the children to a game in PE, in which they have to throw a foam ball between two benches. While the children are actively doing that, you could call out, 'Right, if the ball goes between the benches now, you're out.' This will require speedy adaptation. Then try, 'The rules have changed: the ball has to be thrown over the bench and be caught by a teammate.' And so on. The faster the pace, the more the children get used to the feeling of uncertainty – and of being okay with that feeling.

A classroom-based idea might be:

Ask the children to draw a symmetrical pattern/repeating pattern/simple picture of a house. Shortly after they have made a start, say, 'Oh, by the way, no circles allowed.' After a little longer, say, 'You must include two types of triangle.' This can go on for as many goalpost moves as you like.

Lucy (Year 2) said: 'I don't even know what to do!'
Hannah replied: 'Yes you do, just listen to the change each time.'

## Strength in Neuron Numbers

### Intention(s)

To show the children how a strong network of connections in their brain can be beneficial when completing challenging tasks.

### Resources

A large space.

A device with a camera.

### Activity

Take the children into a large space – outside or into the school hall. Tell them that they are each playing the role of a neuron in the brain. Ask them to get into pairs. This is the first neural connection. Ask them to perform a physical action that's a little tricky, like standing together to form a barrier against an imaginary invader. Next, ask the pairs to each join up with another pair. As a group of four, the barrier becomes more solid and effective.

Increase the group size and allow the children to connect using hands, arms, legs, etc. The barrier becomes more effective with every additional pair of children.

When the whole class is connected, discuss the strength of the barrier. Take a photo and display it in class as a reminder of the idea that the more we connect with other people and ideas, the stronger the outcome.

Harry (Year 1) said: 'We're really strong now because we are all making the barrier and it's like a rock!'

## Halt the Hurry!

Higher-order thinking

EFFORT

### Intention(s)

To teach the children that it is best to slow down and take care, rather than rush our work and miss the opportunity to learn.

### Resources

Drawing materials.

### Activity

The children need to be encouraged to take care with, and have pride in, their work. Those who rush rarely get the most out of a learning experience. Ask the children to close their eyes and build a picture in their mind as you speak to them. You could choose your own imaginary environment, or use the following example:

> I'd like you to imagine walking along a track near a beach. When you reach the beach, you sit down for a few moments and then get up and run around, exploring what you find. What will you do next? What will you play?

Ask the children to draw a picture of what they see in their imaginations. They will all draw something slightly different, but because the imaginary picture you painted was short and rushed, the outcomes will either be very simple or augmented with detail that you didn't provide. When they're done, talk them through the next lengthier, more observant passage:

> I'd like you to imagine that you are walking along a dusty track. The weather is warm and you can hear birds sing-ing in the sky. When you take a step, the tiny, chalky, dry stones on the track crack and crunch under your feet. You walk slowly for a few minutes and then reach a beach. The beach is empty and the only sounds you can hear are

the seagulls calling overhead. You sit down for a moment, looking at the natural beauty of the beach and enjoying the feeling of the sand underneath your legs. You decide to explore. As you walk, you turn around in a full circle, looking in every direction at the majestic surroundings. In the distance to the left, you see a tiny sparkle – a glint in the sunshine. You have no idea what it is, so you walk in the direction of the strange sight. As you get closer, you see that it's the entrance to a cave, half-flooded with seawater, but not so deeply that you can't wade in. You suddenly realise that the cave is filled with boxes of jewels, gold bars and silver figurines. The glint in the sunshine was a gold coin, which had been transported to the opening of the cave by the tide. You know you've found a lifetime's worth of treasure. You now need to decide what you're going to do next.

This imagery will encourage much more detail in their pictures. Discuss how when we hurry, we miss out on so much. When we take our time, we notice so much more, and take so much more in.

Jason (Year 6) said: 'This is like when you're on holiday and you have more time to enjoy things because you don't have to do much at all.'

## What on Earth is This Word?

 Challenge  Higher-order thinking

| Intention(s) | Activity |
|---|---|
| To develop higher-order thinking and questioning skills. | At the beginning of any new topic, give the children a bank of about 15 words. Some they should know already, some they might have a sense of the meaning and some should be challenging words that they probably won't have come across. |
| **Resources**<br>Word banks. | Model using the question words (what, which, who, how, why, etc.) for the children. They then have to explain the words they definitely know, and devise questions to check their knowledge of the words they think they might know and work out the meaning of the ones they don't know. |
| | Dissect the process and talk about how the children are working out their own ways to augment their knowledge and vocabulary. The crux of the lesson is that even if they don't know something at the start, they can use their higher-order thinking and questioning skills to power their knowledge acquisition. |

Esmay (Year 4) said: 'This was good in maths because I realised that we all know different words, and that's okay.'

## Bridge the Learning

Higher-order
thinking

### Intention(s)

To show
the children
how to make
connections
in their
learning.

### Resources

The bridge
graphic,
reproduced
large enough
so the
children can
write in the
boxes.

Pens.

### Activity

This is an ongoing activity that you can do whenever you
want to encourage the children to make connections in their
learning. The more they make connections, the more they will
develop creative thinking skills and their ability to make sense
of the unknown. If we can build the tendency to link learning,
then nothing new is a feared unknown. It's a bit like playing
word association, but looking at their real-life learning.

Your bridge should look something like this:

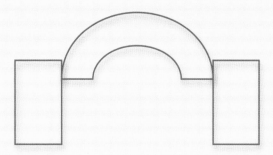

In the left-hand box, help the children to write or draw what
they have done in the morning – for example, counting to 10.
In the right-hand box they can add a piece of learning from
later in the day – for example, mixing different colours. In the
middle of the bridge, the children need to find a way of linking
the two together. For example, they might decide to write 'The
numbers 1–5 could be blue, and the numbers 6–10 could be
red. There would be the same amount of blue and red.' This

could be adapted to make more abstract links in Key Stage 2; you may even get similes and other creative links on the bridge part.

Alessandro (Reception) said: 'There is something the same about the day for me.'

## What's a Teacher? What's a Learner? Part 1

Higher-order thinking    Collaboration

| Intention(s) | Activity |
|---|---|
| To get the children to use the language of teaching and learning. To teach metacognitive skills. | This lesson uses some of the principles of metacognition.<br><br>To warm up, start off with the children on their feet. They walk around the room and name all of the objects they can see – this is getting them confident with speaking out and reinforcing that the names of objects are nouns. Then make the game increasingly more challenging – for example, by using adjectives with the nouns. Then they have to go around and say what the objects are *not*. It's not a banana, etc. (The teacher could model how to do this first.) The children could then work out their own criteria for further rounds. |
| Resources<br><br>None. | Then ask the children to get into pairs and name themselves A and B. They will construct a debate on the topic 'What's more important: holidays or term time?' Partner A will debate one perspective, and B will argue the other point of view. Give the children some sentence stems to help scaffold their arguments. Then they can join up with another pair – A's working together on one side and B's working on the counterargument – to debate: 'What's worse, not doing homework or not doing work in school?' Listen in and jot down their ideas on the board to |

discuss later. Now that the children have learnt this skill, they can face each other in two opposing lines – A's on one side, B's on the other. They now have to debate the question, 'What's more important, a good teacher or a good learner?' Pose questions throughout the debate. At the end, the children can choose a side to support – teaching or learning. Explore the ideas that come out of the discussion.

Vinny (Year 6) said: 'We're all teachers and we're all learners. A teacher could even learn from a learner!'

## What's a Teacher? What's a Learner? Part 2

Higher-order thinking    Collaboration

### Intention(s)

To encourage the children to take an active role in their learning, and not rely on the teacher as an imparter of knowledge.

### Resources

Pens and poster paper (which you could cut out into

### Activity

With the discussion from Part 1 fresh in their minds, the children can record some of their ideas for a display. On their own, children complete the sentence 'I think learning is ...' Then in pairs, they address 'We think teaching is ...' Lastly, in groups of four, they explore 'We think the difference between teaching and learning is ...' They can write down their best ideas to add to the display.

The children are learning about metacognition, and this activity serves as a reminder that they are instrumental in their own learning. It's not up to the teacher to impart knowledge to them; it's an organic cycle between the children and the teachers – everyone learns, and everyone teaches. Consequently, the children place importance

thought bubbles if you wanted to).

on their roles as learners, and develop the motivation to self-regulate.

Tommy (Year 6) said: 'We do this as a team. Nobody can learn or teach without someone else.'

## Flipping Out

Explicit growth mindset

| Intention(s) | Activity |
|---|---|
| To introduce the workings of the brain to the children. | This will help the children to learn how neurons fire and wire together when we learn something new. It's quite fiddly and takes a lot of patience. Model the following process and then give the materials to the children for them to have a go. |
| **Resources** | Use a packet of sticky notes. Draw a very simple neuron on the last note in the pack. Sticky notes are good because you can just about see through them in order to draw over the outline of the image on the note underneath (you could use tracing paper or a notebook with thin pages instead). On the next note, draw over your existing neuron, and add some flashing sparks coming out of it. Turn to the next note, trace over the existing picture and draw a synapse ready for a new neuron. After this, add a new neuron, and continue until the top page shows a network of neurons that has been built up page by page. |
| Packs of sticky notes. Pencils. A picture of a neuron for reference. | |
| | The children will see how firing neurons eventually lead to a bigger network, and a better-connected brain. |

Luke (Year 3) said: 'I've done it now. Shall I help someone else?'

The following nine lessons relate to the central hook of this book – Stuck Island, which we need to get off if we are to swim in Challenge Ocean. You could decide to treat this as a complete unit of work or mini-topic, but the possibilities for integrating it into art, science, English and PSHE are endless. Feel free to pick and choose individual lessons that you feel will be appropriate for your class. If you think of Stuck Island as the starting point in the growth-mindset journey, then these lessons can help to embed and develop the children's understanding of what growth mindset is all about. Each activity will provide another connection in their web of understanding.

## Welcome to the Island

Explicit growth mindset

| Intention(s) | Activity |
| --- | --- |
| To introduce the island analogy. | Introduce the children to a simple desert island, which they have found themselves transported to. It's lovely and peaceful, but quite sparse. Ask them to list all the wonderful things about being on that island. Help the children to see the island as being comfortable, serene and peaceful. |
| **Resources** | They could write a passage of descriptive writing, using a range of adjectives to describe what they see, hear, feel, smell and taste. Link this to science and the senses. Alternatively, they could write a description of the island as a story setting. Play some music to complement the feel of the island. |
| Music. | |
| An image of Stuck Island. | Now it's time to explore the analogy. The island is their comfortable place in learning. A place where they get everything right, and don't feel any stress. Work is easy and is completed without much effort. Help the children to relate this analogy to a subject area or piece of work which is fresh in |

their memory. Tease out the analogy so they can structure their thinking with the help of real-life examples.

William (Year 2) said: 'I feel like that when I'm doing adding because it's easy and I can do it in my head.'

## Aren't There Any Flowers Here?

| Intention(s) | Activity |
| --- | --- |
| To realise that staying in one comfortable place in their learning won't lead to fulfilment. | What would it be like on day ten of living on the island? Ask the children what might be irritating them by then. What would you miss? Don't you wish you could see a few flowers growing on the island? |
| | Ask them to write a diary entry or postcard. Lead the children to the conclusion that it's time to leave the island, and discuss how it isn't going to be easy. How will you leave? What direction are you meant to go in? What might be in the ocean? The diary entry could describe the challenges of leaving the comfortable island. The children know that they can't stay there forever, but the decision to leave is scary. |
| **Resources** | |
| General classroom resources. | |
| | Share some of the diary entries. Do all the children have the same concerns? Why? Why not? Discuss individuality and how we all find different things and feelings tricky. |
| | Here the analogy is that it's all very well being comfortable in our learning, but it is unsatisfying in the end. We have to leave our comfort zone if we want to better ourselves. |

Lewis (Year 4) said: 'Dear Diary, it's been lovely and relaxing, but now I need something to get my teeth into. There isn't enough here for me.'

## Danger: Crabs!

| Intention(s) | Activity |
|---|---|
| To help the children accept the fear of something tricky or unknown as a challenge to be overcome. | Now that we have made the decision to leave Stuck Island, we look into the water and find that there are little crabs nipping away by the shoreline. Discuss the children's experiences of crabs at the seaside. Are they harmful? They might make us feel a little scared but we can overcome that with a bit of bravery. |
| | The crabs represent a challenge or a scary prospect. We know that with some strength of mind, we can wade through the water and get past the crabs with little or no worry for our well-being. But they are still there, posing a bit of a threat. New learning is just the same, as is tackling something tricky. |
| Resources | You could draw some crabs to add to your growth mindset display. In their claws, they could hold notes about something that the children found a bit daunting, but decided to wade in and try anyway. |
| Paper and pens. | |

Emily (Year 5) said: 'My brother was scared of the crabs at the beach. I showed him how to pick one up and then he wanted to pick them all out of the bucket when we'd caught some during crab fishing!'

## That Sinking Feeling

RESILIENCE    Challenge    EFFORT    Explicit growth mindset

### Intention(s)

To help the children understand the feelings of helplessness and failure, and learn strategies to overcome them.

### Resources

Sand, glue, poster paper and pens.

### Activity

We've braved the crabs and survived the first challenge, and everything looks a bit more interesting now. We can see further into the distance and more of the landscape. Now introduce the quicksand. This is the sinking feeling we get when everything gets a bit difficult, and we feel like nothing will help. It's a feeling of helplessness.

Have a discussion about the strategies we use when we find something tricky in school. We can:

- Ask a friend for advice.
- Look in a book.
- Remember content from previous lessons.
- Talk to the teacher.
- Work in a group to discuss and solve the problem.
- Give ourselves some time and space and come back to the problem a little later.

Create some sand art – spread glue onto poster paper and sprinkle sand onto it. The children could make warning signs about the quicksand and give emergency lifesaving tips for others. This could be put on display as a permanent reference point for the children.

Role play scenarios in which the children feel like they will never understand something, and use the techniques you've discussed and formulated as a class to get everyone out.

The quicksand represents those times when you have tried to overcome a challenge but end up feeling like you are sinking and have no way of escaping. The quicksand drags you down and you feel like trying with the work is hopeless.

Duncan (Year 3) said: 'How about asking someone who looks like they are confident?'

## Shark Attack!

RESILIENCE

Explicit growth mindset

| Intention(s) | Activity |
|---|---|
| To learn strategies to help the children take the plunge into the challenge, as they know it'll provide new excitement. | Introduce the children to the following poem. Dissect it and look at the language. What are the themes? What lessons does it contain? |

> I see it lurking in the deep,
>
> It's eerie, and blue and grey.
>
> Floating, gliding, cutting the water,
>
> People get out of its way.
>
> I feel the fear, I know it's a shark,
>
> I imagine the teeth and the bite.
>
> I'd better run. *Avoid! Avoid!*
>
> My body freezes with fright.

## Resources

A copy of the poem (this is available as a downloadable resource at www.crownhouse.co.uk/featured/learning-without-fear).

Paper and pens for noting ideas.

But then I look. I truly look,

I try to make sense of this beast.

There's something amiss and I need to be sure,

Does it really want us as its feast?

I notice the rounded nose on its face.

Then braver, I feel quite alright.

It's swimming much closer to me, and it's calm,

There aren't any teeth – and no bite!

What fools we have been! The relief's like a hug,

A dolphin – all ready to smile.

We were scared and nearly missed out on this swim.

A dolphin it was all the while.

Get the children to create actions to go with the poem and learn it (or an extract) by heart. Perform it to an audience and ask the children to explain the moral.

The sharks represent work that we will not even try because we assume something negative – it's too hard, it doesn't interest me, I won't understand what to do, etc. Assuming means that we don't even get to see whether we are correct in our belief or not. So, if we assume it's a shark, we'll never realise that it's actually a dolphin and that we are missing out on something wonderful.

Lillie (Year 6) said: 'When I think something is horrid, I sometimes count to ten and make sure I breathe properly. Then it calms me down and I can try thinking about it again.'

## The Deep, Deep Ocean

Challenge    EFFORT    Explicit growth mindset

### Intention(s)

To encourage the children to appreciate depth in their learning.

### Resources

Video clips and images of under the sea.

Internet-enabled devices.

### Activity

Show the children a video clip of a deep-sea diver, and all the interesting things they can see underwater. Discuss and make a list of the things the children spot.

Have any of the children been swimming in the sea? What did they see when they were swimming on the surface? Help the children to realise that you only get to see wonderful underwater things when you make yourself dive deeper. It's the same with learning – if you only do the minimum, you don't get to see the wonderful things in the deep part of the learning.

Allow the children to find an underwater picture on the internet to use as a stimulus for free writing. The children may like to:

- Write a description of it.
- Label it.
- Draw it.
- Use it as a story stimulus.
- Create a backstory for why whatever is in the picture is there.
- Create some sound effects.
- Write a poem about it.
- List adjectives that match the setting.

Taylor (Year 4) said: 'That diver is lucky to see all those things. We don't have them in our sea.'

## Exciting Horizons

### Intention(s)

For the children to understand the benefit of embracing the wider world of learning and opportunity.

### Resources

Examples of landscape paintings.

Art materials.

### Activity

Look at some landscape paintings. Works by Thomas Doughty, David Johnson and John Constable are good examples, and are readily available online.

How does the artist create the horizon? What is on the horizon? Discuss how horizons are the furthest thing we can see and aren't always clear. This makes them unknown and exciting.

Teach the children how to create landscape colour washes. Then add some foreground detail and, finally, add something unknown and exciting on the horizon. Make the analogy with their learning – it's exciting when it's not completely clear what's ahead, because we have the chance to find out.

Jemma (Year 5) said: 'When I started ballet lessons, I wasn't sure how long I would carry on for. I really liked it though, and now I'm starting to work for my first award.'

## Survival Kit

RESILIENCE collaboration

Explicit growth mindset

### Intention(s)

For the children to build a personal toolbox of skills to support a growth mindset.

### Resources

Objects from the survival kit, or pictures of them.

### Activity

Return to the quicksand, and remember the feelings associated with it. In daily life, what physical tools do we use to help us?

Introduce children to the survival kit pictures (these are available as downloadable resources at www.crownhouse.co.uk/featured/learning-without-fear).

It's likely you won't have all these resources lying around, so pictures of the objects will suffice. Discuss the items, and then allow the children to use them in imaginative role play. In small groups, the children can create tableaux or dramatic short sketches to demonstrate the help that these resources can offer during a piece of challenging work.

Denny (Reception) said: 'A lifeguard looks at the swimmers to see if they are okay and if they need help.'

## The Wider Islands

Explicit growth
mindset

| Intention(s) | Activity |
|---|---|
| To link the children's learning with other tangible situations. | Add pictures of Stuck Island to your growth mindset display. Whenever you notice that someone has used the techniques taught during the island lessons, ask them to sign their name next to the relevant picture. |
| | This can also be reinforced when you read stories in which the characters are in situations that link to the island analogy. Make notes on the display each time you see these parallels, and the children will soon see how growth mindset threads through all areas of the curriculum and their learning. |
| **Resources** | |
| Display materials. | |

Violetta (Reception) said: 'That character is doing what we do with the goggles!' (referring to a character in her home reading book).

# Chapter 11
# ASSESSING THE IMPACT OF YOUR ENDEAVOUR

We hope that by the time you get to this point in your journey of embedding growth mindset you'll feel like you've completed your brief. Hopefully it'll be running through all that the children do, and how they feel about their learning lives. It's useful, though, to take stock and see just how much difference it's made. Maybe you need to qualify all your hard work for senior leaders in your school. Perhaps you're so inspired that you want to spread the word, but need to have the facts to hand in order to sell the idea to your busy colleagues.

Like any measure in schools, you'll need to look at several sources to get a clear picture of impact. It won't be obvious just from talking to children because – if your endeavours have been successful – they'll speak the language of growth mindset and will know exactly what you want to hear. It's all about watching them *walk the walk* rather than *talk the talk*. Consider what you do when you want to assess progress in maths: you look in books, assess for learning in lessons, listen to the children's oral responses, consider their scores in summative assessments and look at the work they produce in informal situations. Growth mindset doesn't need to be any different; there'll be evidence wherever you look.

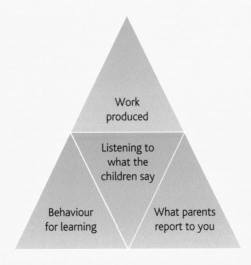

# WORK PRODUCED

The signs that your children have achieved a positive shift in mindset will show in the work they produce. You might see:

- An increase in written output because they are willing to have a go and are not fearing negative judgement. Stamina for writing will improve because they start to enjoy the process of creating, rather than trying to finish a piece of work as quickly as they can.

- Children making more creative and willingly experimental attempts with grammatical structures and difficult words – they try to make their writing more skilful without worrying that it may not be totally grammatically accurate.

- More creativity in lessons because they are confident in their own self and style.

- An increase in independence during tasks. It's all about moving away from *copying* someone else during collaboration, to *developing ideas with* someone else. When it comes to independent work, they don't fear being left alone.

- A willingness to try trickier work. One of the most wonderful things about developing a growth mindset is that it encourages the children to start welcoming the trickier tasks rather than the easier ones. When you lay out your resources and the children choose their own differentiated task, it's marvellous when they try something slightly harder than what you would have chosen for them. It's the same joy that comes with ditching ability grouping. The children can be in charge of their own limits, and when they have developed their growth mindset, they will find it far more appealing to reach higher rather than lower. It's the wonderful surprises that this brings that get us through the tougher times.

# LISTENING TO WHAT THE CHILDREN SAY

Growth mindset should permeate the children's whole outlook. When they truly embrace it, growth mindset will be in all their conversations, showing most frequently as positivity and a willingness to try.

- When children are talking to other children, there'll be encouragement. 'Try doing it this way', or 'You can do it'. They will celebrate what others are doing, and point out their successes. With the seven statements of growth mindset on the wall, I've overheard children saying to each other 'You're doing loads of number 6 today'. They refer to them, and they become part of the conversation.

- When they talk to you, you'll see an increase in self-esteem. There will still be children who say that they can't do something, but it'll become less common, and others will hopefully chip in with a technique to dilute that way of thinking. For example, Benjamin might say, 'I just can't do this type of multiplication.' In response, Eloise might reply, 'How about if you set it out like this? That'll make it clearer and you'll be able to see the tens and the ones in the columns.' In our classrooms, children have got into the habit of writing short messages at the end of their work, to let us know how they feel about their achievement, or the process of completing it. It's a lovely way to let the pupils have a voice, and their messages will let you in on whether the growth mindset environment has had an impact. Here's one that Megan wrote to Julia recently: 'I feel amazing because you can be imaginative. Also if the teacher helps you, it's their idea, not yours.' It shows where her mindset lies at that particular time, and what we still need to work on in order for her to grow further.

- What do the children say when they're outside the classroom? Reports of arguments in the playground or corridor can give you a truthful window into their mindset. If you listen when the children think you're not, you'll hear their truer feelings.

# BEHAVIOUR FOR LEARNING

If we see growth mindset as a way of being – an aspect of personality – then the children's behaviour will express a great deal. Children with a growth mindset are ready to learn and enjoy a challenge. We'd see that translated into behaviour for learning. Children would show:

- A readiness to listen. Children will contribute to achieving tighter transitions between playtime and lessons, or between lessons. They'll want to get started, and they'll be excited about what they are about to 'gain' from the next session.

- Less tolerance for others' undesirable behaviour. Your pupils will see disruption to lessons as a waste of their time. There isn't anything to be won by messing about because to someone with a growth mindset, messing about is giving away the chance to learn something.

- Respect for the school environment. They will want to contribute to making things better, rather than ruin the result of someone else's work or effort.

- An appreciation for other children's successes. If children are all striving to be the best that they can be, and achieving more as a result, then there is no need to be envious or resentful of others' successes. Children will start to be inspired by the greatness of others, rather than seeing it as a threat. If success is a result of hard work and effort, then children will be encouraged that they could reach that point too.

# WHAT PARENTS REPORT TO YOU

When it comes to parents' evenings, open evenings or end of year report time, your conversations with parents and carers can be a rich bed of information about how successful you've been in shifting their child's mindset. If they've developed a growth mindset, they'll be showing it in their out of school activities. Parents will be dropping them off at the far gate instead of the classroom door, because their child will be ready, willing and excited to come into school. Parents might even report that their child has been explaining the formal written method of subtraction to them, all because the child wants their parent to have a light-bulb moment too! It's great when you see:

- A willingness to separate from their parents each morning.

- A carefree welcome when they are picked up after a day when they found a certain lesson tricky. They know that it means they have been challenged and are moving on in their learning, rather than signalling failure.

- Parents speaking positively about their child's confidence and attitude towards homework.

- Parents talking about the new activities, hobbies and challenges the child has tried out.

When you're sitting quietly, think about the difference between September and now. Look back at the staff questionnaire from Chapter 2. You might like to complete it again and compare your results. Or, now that you are more consciously aware of the aspects of growth mindset, you could have a look at the following. We're more ready for these statements now that we're fully clued up.

## Teacher reflection tool

Where would you place your class (use the principle of best fit) on these sliding scales?

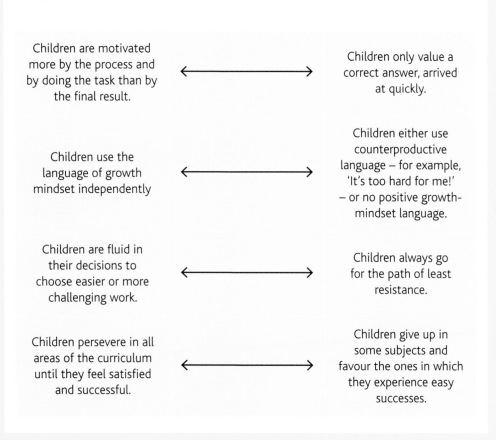

| | |
|---|---|
| Children are motivated more by the process and by doing the task than by the final result. | Children only value a correct answer, arrived at quickly. |
| Children use the language of growth mindset independently | Children either use counterproductive language – for example, 'It's too hard for me!' – or no positive growth-mindset language. |
| Children are fluid in their decisions to choose easier or more challenging work. | Children always go for the path of least resistance. |
| Children persevere in all areas of the curriculum until they feel satisfied and successful. | Children give up in some subjects and favour the ones in which they experience easy successes. |

Depending on your reflection, you might clearly see where you have work to do. It may be that certain areas of growth mindset are strong. Maybe the children's openness to facing a challenge is still weak? Have a look through the lesson ideas for ones that relate to an area you feel your class still needs to work on. That idea could then be adapted to give you some additional options for activities to remedy any gaps. Hopefully there'll be areas of success that could be shared with other teachers in your year group or phase. Sharing what works best will always be a great way to spread the positivity of growth mindset around the school.

When it comes to the children, it's a great idea to watch them show you whether they've grasped the concept. Depending on their personality traits, questionnaires sometimes skew the children towards the 'right' answers. They might realise what you're trying to achieve and give you the answer they think you want to hear. Putting children into a scenario in which a growth mindset would change the outcome is one way to see a more honest result. Choose one of the lesson ideas from Chapter 10 and simply see how they respond. Though it'll be tempting to dissect and discuss the unfolding conversations, look at it as an opportunity to just sit back and watch. What you learn will show you how far your children have come.

The sequence of photos that follows helped Julia assess her impact on her then five-year-old son, James (the one with the terribly fixed mindset before). She says *before* because the event we're about to describe thrilled the bones of her own growth mindset and her aspirations for his.

James had never attempted the monkey bars before. He was reticent, and perhaps a bit too young. But he quoted from the Stead family motto, and had a go. Tick number one!

He needed to make a few attempts with Julia holding his weight to get a feel for the motion.

Then he tried it alone.

He felt a bit safer and more confident.

He became sure that he could do more, but lost his grip and fell hard (his face was left with an imprint of the ground on it).

After dusting himself down, he got straight back up, to persevere without fear of another fall.

He eventually got to the fourth rung. The resilience that Julia had hoped to see for months had shown up. He was proud of himself for not giving up, and for trying again using what he'd learnt from each go. It's situations like these that we want you to look out for – you can find them every day in your classroom.

## Chapter 12

# LOOKING FURTHER AFIELD: ENGAGING PARENTS

Take this calculation:

There are 8,760 hours in a year.

An average school day in the UK is from 8.50am to 3.15pm, which is 6 hours and 25 minutes.

Children attend school for 190 days a year, or 1,219 hours.

There are 7,541 hours left in the year in which children are at home or somewhere else outside of school.

This means that they spend 86% of their time at home, and only 14% of their time at school.

If we want to be even more accurate, we can take account of when children are likely to be asleep (10 hours a night), and we arrive at the following totals:

Children spend 3,891 waking hours at home out of 5,110 waking hours in a year.

Therefore, parents and carers get 76% of children's waking hours, while teachers get the remaining 24%.

The National Research Council in the United States arrived at the same percentages of time spent with teachers and parents, and, furthermore, they state: 'Engendering parent support for the core learning principles and parent involvement in the learning process is of utmost importance.'[1] Julia felt very vindicated when she read this, as she'd originally worked out the calculation herself – she'd taken the trickier path rather than relying on someone else's maths brain!

---

1   National Research Council, *How People Learn: Brain, Mind, Experience, and School: Expanded Edition* (Washington, DC: National Academies Press, 2000), p. 26. Available at: https://doi.org/10.17226/9853.

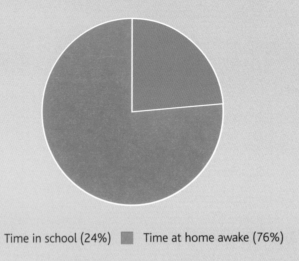

Time in school (24%)  Time at home awake (76%)

Percentage of children's waking hours spent at home versus at school

Although, as teachers, we are undoubtedly one of the main influences on a child's developing brain, we can only directly influence just under a quarter of the time during which they are conscious. So it's easy to see why parents, families and friends play such a huge role in forming who children are, what they become and how their emergent personalities develop.

With this in mind, we can see the importance of engaging parents in everything we do in school. If we want to have a big impact by embedding growth mindset in all areas of school life, it would be crazy to ignore the remaining 76% of children's waking hours. Without getting everyone on board, we're undermining our efforts to introduce real, lasting change in the children's mindsets, and our chances of impacting on their future success.

How many times have you heard statements like the following real-life examples from parents? We've actually heard these gems over the past academic year and wrote them down for the purposes of this book as they were so illustrative.

I'm no good at maths – she gets it from me!

He doesn't like writing because he can't do cursive letters.

I've always said she'll be a carer or work in a shop.

I hated reading at school too. He's like me. I haven't read since I left school.

He just can't draw to save his life!

When we hear this, inside we are screaming, 'You're making them like that by saying things like this!' The professional Julia and Ruchi try hard to smile sympathetically and to explain that their child is their own person with the capacity to learn anything – including to enjoy anything they choose. It's not always easy, as you know. Again, we can relate this to the Pygmalion effect, and see how parental expectations become the child's version of normal – their status quo. Low parental expectations may seem easy to fulfil to the child, but we want them to aim higher in an attempt to increase their capacity for self-fulfilment. Rather than simply disregard these kinds of conversations, we need to pass on information about growth mindset – and our experiences with it – and allow parents to see just how valuable it is. Parents are our pupils' role models. Children hear their language, see their actions and grow up emulating what they see. The importance of role models knowing the effect that they are having is clear. So the million-pound question remains: how do we engage the parents?

We've seen schools resort to withholding reports and only giving them out at an information evening about a particular strategy that they want parents on board with, or incentivising attendance at information events using wine and chocolates. While somewhat desperate, it does go to show that we are keen to find ways to engage parents and get them into the building to listen to what we have to say. We know the value in it, but it's sharing the value with the parents that is sometimes challenging.

We've found it useful to create a list of all the opportunities we have for contact with parents in our day-to-day lives at school. We came up with the following:

- At the door in the morning or at the end of the day.

- In-class sessions for parents.

- Start of year drop-ins.

- Parents' evenings.

- Celebration events and assemblies.

- Letters home.

- School newsletters.

- Reports.

- Homework.

If there are so many opportunities to communicate with parents, it's just a case of choosing the most realistic and effective ones through which to sell the message of growth mindset.

## THE POWER OF LETTERS HOME

It seems obvious to start with letters home. It's a cheap and easy way to say all that you want to say, and it allows parents to access the information at a time that's convenient for them. The letter needs to contain all the essential information – imagining that you've got a two-minute block of the parents' attention might help you to focus on the three key points, which are:

1.  What a growth mindset looks like.

2. Why it's important.

3. How parents can help their child develop one.

You might like to use the following text, adapt it or even create your own now that you know all about growth mindset.

## What a growth mindset looks like

Growth mindset is a term that describes the way in which people see their ability and intelligence. Children with a fixed mindset tend to think that intelligence is decided and unchangeable – if something is tricky or hard, then the best idea is to leave it and do something that they're good at instead. However, children with a growth mindset see challenge as a positive thing, because it means they are learning something new and getting better.

A growth mindset allows children to learn from their mistakes and find new ways of doing things. They learn from other people and collaborate to find effective ways to solve problems. The growth-mindset approach teaches us that children are not born with a natural talent which means they can achieve and be successful; there is a journey to success. Effort and hard work are key.

When we face a challenge, the brain makes new connections – the brain is actually growing through these new experiences. Children with a growth mindset are resilient and are not put off a task just because they don't immediately see a solution. As a school, we believe that these skills set children up for a love of learning and a successful life, full of new challenges, experiences and strategies.

## Why it's important

A growth mindset develops desirable characteristics in your child – such as resilience, collaboration, effort, determination and the ability to problem-solve. We want our children to show these kinds of traits throughout their lives – it stands them in good stead for whatever comes their way. As a school, we want to see children applying these traits to their learning.

Our business is in growing brains, growing children's abilities and helping them to develop into interested lifelong learners who are always ready for the next challenge or adventure. We see having a growth mindset as a gold-plated tool to help us achieve this.

Our mindsets can change, even when we're adults, so we'd like to tell you about the benefits of having a growth mindset. Please come into school to see for yourself how we help children to develop a growth mindset, and witness the successes it brings!

## How you can help develop growth mindset in your child

**Model making mistakes.** If children see that you embrace making mistakes, they will learn not to fear them. Mistakes help us to learn, because if we try again we can learn to avoid that mistake and use a different strategy instead. Celebrating mistakes as a tool to help us grow and learn puts them in a positive light, and helps to encourage children to be resilient and try again.

**Celebrate positive role models.** Point out people in your child's life who have worked hard to achieve something good. Show children that it's effort, determination and hard work that result in success. Start conversations about your child's favourite sports star, for example – there isn't one athlete out there who's topped the league without a lifetime of effort.

**A warning about siblings.** When dealing with siblings, try not to place importance on rivalry and competition. Value the process of taking part in sports or activities rather than who gets the trophy at the end.

**Language.** Be careful about the messages you're giving your child. Saying things like, 'You get your lack of coordination from me' or 'That's too tricky for little boys' can lead to a fixed notion of what they can and cannot do, and they will fit in to the picture you paint for them. It's a self-fulfilling prophecy – if you aim high with the expectation that they can do tricky things, your child will inflate their effort to meet those expectations.

**Praise.** Praising children by saying things like 'You're a natural' or 'That's so easy for you, well done' can give children the impression that their success is down to natural talent only – and it follows that if they don't have that innate talent, they will be unsuccessful. Understanding *how* they can succeed is key. If children only value praise for doing something successfully, they are likely to give up if they face difficulty in the future. Praising the effort or the strategy they used helps children to understand that hard work is the key to success, and that they can therefore be successful at anything if they work for it.

**Recommended reading.** (Here you would need to add a reading list based on your individual school's activities. A good starting point would be the suggestions for books to use in class that we've included in the references and further reading section.)

**Recommended online sources.** (Here you would need to add a list of any websites that you have found helpful in your school's mindset journey. For example, we'd recommend the BBC's page: http://www.bbc.co.uk/cbeebies/grownups/help-your-child-try-new-things.)

## BROADENING YOUR REACH

The letter could go home as a stand-alone document or as a take-away from an information session which parents are invited to attend in person. We've always found that providing an information session at the start or end of the school day encourages parents to attend. That way they don't have to come back to school again at 7pm when it's raining and it's tempting not to bother. It's easier to sell the event to the staff who have to attend it too! Do consider, though, those parents who can only attend school events outside of standard full-time working hours.

An information session gives you a captive audience in the school hall, with the opportunity to sell your ideas with a speech and presentation that says exactly what you want parents to know. You could use the information letter as a foundation from which to elaborate further, giving parents a deeper understanding of the concepts. Giving the letter out at the end would help to cement the ideas, and if you encourage parents to take one for absent friends, the word might spread more effectively. A more far-reaching – although inevitably more diluted – option could be to include a growth mindset 'thought for the week' in your school newsletter. The characteristics of growth mindset could be shared as a regular feature in each newsletter, and you could also share some of the inspiring quotes you'll use with the children. This would serve to remind parents that growth mindset is alive, well and continuing indefinitely in their child's school.

As a parent, Julia would like to think that if she didn't already know what a positive impact she could have on her child by implementing features of growth mindset in her family's home life, she'd jump at the chance if offered by school. (Of course, her aware-ness of this as a teacher has already had an impact on her role as a parent, as we saw with James' success on the monkey bars at the end of Chapter 11.) She'd value knowing how she could change her own life too. Giving parents this information isn't just for the children's benefit – it can enrich parents' experiences as well.

Do you have time for a quick anecdote? One day – during the period in which we were writing this book – Julia was walking round Bury St Edmunds, talking to her mum about how she'd like her son, James, to learn to play the piano. Julia described how a piano might just fit into a specific corner of the lounge, and then said: 'I wish I could learn too, but my brain is wired up the wrong way and I just can't do it.' She stopped, aghast at what she'd just said and hoping that James hadn't heard. It was a totally fixed mindset way of thinking. Even as someone who now lives and breathes growth mindset, she still has to watch her language. What she really meant was that she finds it tricky to coordinate both hands if they are doing different things at the same time. If she had lessons, she'd no doubt develop this skill. Her brain isn't fixed, and her skill level can improve with hard work – which is true of everyone. How much better would it be for parents to feel that way, rather than looking at a piano and admitting defeat before even considering having a lesson. Watch that mummy-mouth, Julia! That was, however, balanced by a wonderful chat between James and his dad, which resulted in James placing so much importance on the idea of a family motto that he created the following (with spelling support from his dad!):

Stead motos
_____

1 Astead never gives up.

2 A stead always tries his best

3 Astead loves a challenge

As you'll have already seen, for growth mindset culture to flourish in a school, the messages have to be consistent across the whole community. This includes all pupils, teachers and parents. When we implement a whole-school initiative, the messages that parents see need to be consistent and clear. The old 'if I had a pound for each time a parent ...' adage comes into play here. You can probably think of occasions when parents have complained about a member of staff applying the behaviour policy very differently – and in their eyes, unfairly – with two different children. Consistency is key and this also goes for growth mindset. If we are praising effort and determination, rather than a naturally achieved and easily won end result, then we need to be consistent in our explanation of our praise. If it's important to you as a school, you need to make sure that all staff are rewarding growth mindset traits in a fair and consistent way. This leads us on nicely to our next opportunity to engage parents.

## Celebration assemblies

We all know the type: merit assemblies, house point reward assemblies, good work assemblies, etc. The names differ, but the rationale is the same. Parents are invited in to see their child receive an award for something – usual examples include attendance, excellent achievement, progress or a certain number of house points. Lovely. The parents' faces are a delight. But if you're on the journey to embed growth mindset in your whole-school environment, you may want to reconsider. Look back at Chapter 8 and consider the main points – we need to celebrate effort, determination and resilience, rather than end products. We're throwing away the stickers as an external motivator, not cementing them in our school routines. So if we're celebrating growth-mindset style, we can use these events to show the parents what it's all about: our language, content and examples from the children will educate them about the ideals we are aspiring to.

The same attention needs to be paid at parents' evenings and in written reports. The way we phrase things will lead parents to a greater understanding of why we've adopted a growth-mindset approach in school. Consider these very common teacher–parent meeting phrases, and see how we can engage the parents – even if it's covertly – with how we praise and report on their child.

| Instead of | Try saying |
|---|---|
| Sadie really enjoys RE because she's good at understanding others' points of view. | Sadie has listened well to others' ideas in RE and has become skilled in appreciating that people are different. She gets pleasure from understanding these differences. |
| Sadie is more confident in maths than in English because she finds it easier and is good at arriving at answers. | Sadie gets excited about maths because she fully understands the calculation strategies that she's learnt this year. She enjoys the feeling that she gets when she goes from hearing |

| | about a new concept for the first time to finally mastering it. |
|---|---|
| Sadie has a tendency to give up with spellings she finds tricky and often uses a different word that she knows how to spell instead. | Sadie's next step in spelling is to sound out the phonemes that she can hear when she says the word. We are encouraging her to have a go even if she's unsure. Giving up sometimes means that she doesn't have the opportunity to discuss the correct spelling, or to try and see if she can succeed. |
| Sadie likes competition and does her best to win. However, she sometimes becomes upset if she's not the winner in a PE game or if someone finishes a piece of work faster than she does. | Sadie is sometimes more interested in the goal than in the learning she's undertaking. Her best-quality work happens when she slows down. The more she does this, the more she will see that hard work brings better rewards than a quick, easy finish. |
| Sadie led a team to create a wonderful model Tudor house in DT. She was very proud of her work. | Sadie created a wonderful Tudor house as part of a team in DT. She was the team leader, and helped her team to incorporate everyone's ideas into the model. It was great to hear the team change their plans when they realised that the frame wouldn't be strong enough if it was made purely of paper. |

The growth mindset phrasing does two jobs: it models the kinds of activities we want to see our pupils undertaking and it praises them for acting and learning in that way. Furthermore, it makes the communication with the parent far more detailed, child-focused and personalised. Engaging parents doesn't have to mean explicitly teaching them about the theory – it can be done in the everyday too. When parents are dropping children off in the morning, or collecting them in the afternoon, a quick conversation can be a wonderful opportunity for growth-mindset-led praise and celebration. The younger the children, the more opportunity there is for this, as the teachers in EYFS and Key Stage 1 normally see parents as they dismiss each child. A snippet of face-to-face communication does the same job as clever phrasing in reports. Your audience is captive, loves to chat about their child and can be coached in growth-mindset values through the way in which you shape your conversation.

## Displays are not just for the children

Another everyday part of the school environment is the displays we have up around the building. If you can create a display about growth mindset, that's great. Careful, though, as what we don't want is the generic language of growth mindset being printed, laminated and pinned up, with nobody really understanding why or seeing the effects. We want a really vibrant demonstration of growth mindset in action. Have a look back at Chapter 4 for inspiration. The biggest consideration as far as engaging parents goes is the location. You may want to place the display near the main entrance or the head teacher's office. Or each class could create a small window display, facing outwards so that parents can have a look while they're waiting to collect their child at the end of the day. We particularly like these sneaky ways of encouraging parents to engage without them even realising.

## Parents in the classroom

If you want to make a grander, more obvious gesture to growth mindset, then you could consider introducing 'parents in class' sessions in your school. We have done this, and in our school a teacher took on the initiative as part of a community lead role. Three times a year – once each term – we invite parents to come in and spend 45 minutes with their child in class, experiencing a lesson. This has a few benefits: children love having a parent in class with them as they can show off their skills; parents like to see how their child's teacher actually teaches; parents feel included and listened to as they are asked to complete a questionnaire about parental involvement and what they'd like to see afterwards. The theme changes each term, and all year groups – from nursery to Year 6 – teach to the given theme. When we introduced growth mindset to our school ethos, we used parents in class to demonstrate growth mindset at work, and did a themed growth-mindset lesson in all classes. Julia used the Gappy Wall idea from Chapter 10, all about the brain needing lots of connections to make it strong.

There are lots of times when we come into contact with parents, and they're all opportunities to model what we're selling. How you choose to do so can reflect your intentions and ambitions regarding instilling the culture of growth mindset in all areas of school life. Whether you use explicit channels of communication – like letters home and information sessions – or covert methods – like displays and careful language – the effort you put into communicating the message to parents will ultimately affect how successfully the children change the way in which they think. Teachers are masters of having an impact on the children's lives, but we are only with them for 24% of the time.

# CONCLUSION

As full-time teachers who face all the usual other pressures of life, we completely recognise that finding the time for reading and implementing change in our professional lives is difficult. Anything we endeavour to do almost needs to be vetted for impact before we give it our effort and attention. It was with that thought that this book was designed – we wanted to share tried-and-tested lesson ideas, ready-to-use materials, and (in a medium-sized nutshell) the underpinning theory to back up why understanding mindset is so vital for our pupils.

We have seen how we can introduce growth mindset and positive attitudes to even the very youngest children. For us, it all starts in the run-up to school, when they'll be introduced to learning as a fluid, lifelong endeavour. And *endeavour* is indeed the right word. Learning isn't a linear process of moving from not knowing something to being taught to understanding. It is a wide-ranging and spiralling experience. It grows in different and unpredictable directions as we make connections. It's a way of understanding something a little better, making a link to something we've seen before and maybe even feeling like we realise how little we actually do know. It is so hard to set out in words, that even as we write this paragraph, we see a maze of connections wrestling their way out of our thoughts and onto the page. If we wrote this tomorrow, it could be completely different as different insights and experiences could have come to us in the meantime. We are writing this conclusion in the month of August. In September when we each meet yet another class full of individual brains, we'll make more connections and our understanding could be different again. Our point is that learning is unique to each child, and that's why it doesn't matter whether that individual is a baby, in nursery or ready to leave for secondary school in the summer of Year 6. If they can be encouraged to see learning as a multifaceted way of life and of *being*, they will become more accepting of all the ways in which they can approach the unknown. More importantly, learning will make them feel comfortable, excited and empowered. A child who sees learning as trying out something which might not work at first – as something that can be striven for – will have a mind that's open to learning experiences in all their different forms.

We think you'll know when you have managed to forge a positive growth-mindset culture in your classroom. Children will come in and start working on the task they've been given without sitting and waiting to be spoon-fed the instructions. Ah, the beautiful promises we make! We hope that when you've used the tools in Chapter 11 to measure the impact of your endeavour, you'll be able to see the difference you have made to your children. We hope you'll become a believer in growth mindset, just as we have over the past few years of experimenting with these approaches. You might even want to pass on the gems of what did work to the nay-sayers who have moved on to whatever the new fashionable pedagogy is. What is for sure, though, is that mindset is as much a matter of common sense than it is of anything else, even if we need to inform that common sense to make sure we're filtering the messages that are passed onto our pupils. What is even more true is that fashions come and go, but when you've been teaching for a number of years, you'll see it all come around again. The topic webs of the 1990s are now rewritten, shiny and lauded in classrooms of today. Take these top tips for educators, proposed by a music teacher, Mrs Curwen, in the late nineteenth century:

1.  Teach the easy before the difficult.

2.  Teach the thing before the sign.

3.  Teach one fact at a time, and the commonest fact first.

4.  Leave out all exceptions and anomalies until the general rule is understood.

5.  In training the mind, teach the concrete before the abstract.

6.  In developing physical skill, teach the elemental before the compound, and do one thing at a time.

7.  Proceed from the known to the related unknown.

8.  Let each lesson, as far as possible, rise out of that which goes before, and lead up to that which follows.

9.  Call in the understanding to help the skill at every step.

10. Let the first impression be a correct one; leave no room for misunderstanding.

11. Never tell a pupil anything that you can help him to discover for himself.

12. Let the pupil, as soon as possible, derive some pleasure from his knowledge. Interest can only be kept up by a sense of growth in independent power.[1]

We pride ourselves on engaging with the latest evidence-based research, yet over a century ago, teachers were proposing the very things that we endeavour to do in our contemporary classrooms. In terms of teaching children to have a healthy mindset towards their learning – teaching them to learn without the restrictive bridle of fear – growth mindset will hopefully be around forever. Learning without fear is nothing to do with the latest educational trends or fashions; it's what we are all trying to do in our classrooms every day.

The information we've shared in this book is designed to show you how to help your children see learning as something that needn't be feared. Whether you decide to present the whole theory to the children, simply dip into some lesson ideas to augment an already enabling atmosphere in your classroom or go belt and braces towards a whole new set-up in your classroom and practice, we hope you'll find something you can take away. Perhaps the most valuable thing we can offer is awareness. We've admitted to using fixed-mindset language in the past without giving it a second thought. Our growing awareness has meant that our natural teaching – and parenting – behaviours have become more positive and calm.

An awareness of the impact of mindset has spread to our colleagues. The most recent example of this was during the planning for sports day. Julia's class of Year 5 children proposed some changes to what they thought was an unfair way to organise races. The school had historically ranked children during heats and put them into the sports day races according to their performance. As soon as the conversation began, one child who is always very high-attaining in PE put forward her feelings about this. She felt a pressure to win, she told us, but she also felt for the other children in school. She showed empathy towards those who felt like they'd already been lumped in the 'slow race' and needn't even bother.

It was one of those conversations that made Julia realise how much progress her children had made. These Year 5s were talking like grown-ups, demonstrating an understanding of psychological impact and a desire to improve their experiences. The treasure lay in the whole-class conversation – the talk was all about why the 'speedy' children shouldn't fear losing, and about how the ones in the slower groups could turn the

---

1   Quoted in Jonathan Savage (ed.), *The Guided Reader to Teaching and Learning Music* (Abingdon and New York: Routledge, 2013), pp. 64–65.

experience into a positive in other ways. Still, the children thought it was unfair. There was a staff meeting scheduled after school that evening, and the children in Julia's class wrote ideas about how we could make sports day more conducive to growth mindset. The staff were enlightened, and the format of sports day was changed. Teachers were to group pupils in a way that suited the mindset of the class: it might be random, (with the children *knowing* it was random), or it might be following any other formation that seemed fitting. Ability races became redundant. That the class felt like they had made a change in the school was a gem in their mindset crown. Our awareness of growth mindset – and of racing without fear – changed what can be one of the trickiest days in school for some children into a much more enjoyable experience.

We're all learners. Maybe you've seen aspects of yourself in the personalities of the learners described here. Teachers learn every day, so all our advice applies to us as much as to our pupils. Learning is a way of life, which is manifested in the atmosphere in our classrooms and in our staffrooms.

Learning without fear? Teaching without fear? Living without fear? It can be done, and defeating the fear is the best feeling in the world.

# RESOURCES

Resources are available to download from www.crownhouse.co.uk/featured/learning-without-fear.

Chapter 2

**Staff questionnaire** p. 20

**Key Stage 1 pupil questionnaire** p. 22

**Key Stage 2 pupil questionnaire** p. 23

**'Episodes of watching' prompt paper** p. 26

**Images to accompany mini story 1** p. 28

Anna.jpg Mr Clarke.jpg

**Images to accompany mini story 2** p. 29

Harry.jpg Balancing an egg on a spoon.jpg Anjali.jpg

Harry and Anjali having fun together.jpg

## Images to accompany mini story 3 p. 30

Ali.jpg

Blocks that look a bit like a castle.jpg

Blocks making turrets.jpg

## Images to accompany mini story 4 p. 31

Ellie finds paints.jpg

Ellie paints her name.jpg

Mr Betts looking.jpg

Ellie name better.jpg

Ellie name best.jpg

## Images to accompany mini story 5 p. 32

Majus.jpg

Construction brick car.jpg

Majus worried.jpg

Majus proud.jpg

## Chapter 10 – Resources to use with the Stuck Island analogy

Challenge Ocean.jpg

Compass.jpg

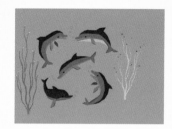

Dolphins.jpg

Driftwood.jpg

Goggles.jpg

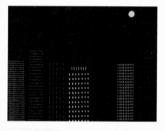

Got-It City stand-alone.jpg

Got-It City with ocean.jpg

I'm stuck.jpg

Learning zone.jpg

Lifeguard tower.jpg

Lifeguard.jpg

Lifejacket.jpg

Rubber ring.jpg

Safe.jpg

Shark infested waters.jpg

SOS flare.jpg

Stuck Island stand-alone.jpg

Stuck Island to Got-It City.jpg

Stuck Island with boy.jpg

Survival kit desk icons.jpg

Underwater diver with text.jpg

Underwater diver.jpg

**Shark Attack! poem** pp. 219–220

# REFERENCES AND FURTHER READING

## BOOKS TO USE WITH THE CHILDREN

Berne, Jennifer (2013). *On a Beam of Light: A Story of Albert Einstein* (San Francisco, California: Chronicle Books).

Bryant, Jen (2013). *A Splash of Red: The Life and Art of Horace Pippin* (New York: Alfred A. Knopf Publishing).

Cook, Julia (2013). *Thanks for the Feedback: My Story About Accepting Criticism and Compliments the Right Way* (Boys Town, NE: Boys Town Press).

Gray, Karlin (2016). *Nadia: The Girl Who Couldn't Sit Still* (New York: Houghton Mifflin Harcourt).

Pett, Mark and Gary Rubenstein (2012). *The Girl Who Never Made Mistakes* (Naperville, IL: Sourcebooks Jabberwocky).

Raschka, Chris (2013). *Everyone Can Learn to Ride a Bicycle* (New York: Schwarz and Wade Books).

Reynolds, Peter H. (2004). *The Dot* (London: Walker Books).

Saltzberg, Barney (2010). *Beautiful Oops* (New York: Workman Publishing).

Sharratt, Nick (2000). *Shark in the Park* (London: Corgi Picture Books).

Spires, Ashley (2017). *The Most Magnificent Thing* (Toronto, ON: Kids Can Press).

Yamada, Kobi (2016). *What Do You Do with a Problem?* (Seattle, WA: Compendium Inc.).

## FURTHER READING

Anderson, Lorin W. and David R. Krathwohl (eds) (2000). *A Taxonomy for Learning, Teaching, and Assessing: A Revision of Bloom's Taxonomy of Educational Objectives* (London: Pearson).

Biggs, John and Kevin Collis (1982). *Evaluating the Quality of Learning: The SOLO Taxonomy* (New York: Academic Press).

Blau, Sheridan D. (2003). *The Literature Workshop: Teaching Texts and Their Readers* (Portsmouth, NH: Heinemann).

Boyd, Pete, Barry Hymer and Karen Lockney (2015). *Learning Teaching: Becoming an Inspirational Teacher* (Northwich: Critical Publishing).

Brown, Peter C., Henry L. Roediger and Mark A. McDaniel (2014). *Make it Stick: The Science of Successful Learning* (Cambridge, MA: Harvard University Press).

Carlton, Martha P. and Adam Winsler (1998). Fostering Intrinsic Motivation in Early Childhood Classrooms, *Early Childhood Education Journal*, 25(3): 159–166. DOI: 10.1023/A:1025601110383

Deci, Edward L. with Richard Flaste (1996). *Why We Do What We Do: Understanding Self-Motivation* (London: Penguin).

Department for Education (2013). *The National Curriculum in England: Key Stages 1 and 2 Framework Document*. Ref: DFE-00178-2013 (London: Department for Education). Available at: https://assets.publishing.service.gov.uk/government/uploads/system/uploads/attachment_data/file/425601/PRIMARY_national_curriculum.pdf.

Diener, Carol I. and Carol S. Dweck (1978). An Analysis of Learned Helplessness: Continuous Changes in Performance, Strategy, and Achievement Cognitions Following Failure, *Journal of Personality and Social Psychology*, 36(5): 451–462.

D'Onfro, Jillian (2015). The Truth About Google's Famous '20% Time' Policy, *Business Insider* (17 April). Available at: https://www.businessinsider.com/google-20-percent-time-policy-2015-4?r=US&IR=T.

Dweck, Carol S. (2006). *Mindset: The New Psychology of Success* (London: Random House).

Eberle, Bob (2008). *Scamper: Games for Imagination Development* (Waco, TX: Prufrock Press).

Elliot, Victoria, Jo-Anne Baird, Therese N. Hopfenbeck, Jenni Ingram, Ian Thompson, Natalie Usher, Mae Zantout, James Richardson and Robbie Coleman (2016). *A Marked Improvement? A Review of the Evidence on Written Marking* (London: Education Endowment Foundation).

Fabian, Hilary and Aline-Wendy Dunlop (2007). *Outcomes of Good Practice in Transition Processes for Children Entering Primary School*. Working Paper 42 (The Hague: Bernard van Leer Foundation).

Fisher, Douglas and Nancy Frey (2009). Feed Up, Back, Forward, *Educational Leadership*, 67(3): 20–25. Available at: http://www.ascd.org/publications/educational-leadership/nov09/vol67/num03/Feed-Up,-Back,-Forward.aspx.

Gross-Loh, Christine (2016). How Praise Became a Consolation Prize, *The Atlantic* (16 December). Available at: https://www.theatlantic.com/education/archive/2016/12/how-praise-became-a-consolation-prize/510845/.

Hanley, Mary, Mariam Khairat, Korey Taylor, Rachel Wilson, Rachel Cole-Fletcher and Deborah M. Riby (2017). Classroom Displays – Attraction or Distraction? Evidence of Impact on Attention and Learning from Children with and without Autism, *Developmental Psychology*, 53(7): 1265–1275. Available at: http://dro.dur.ac.uk/20263/.

Hart, Susan, Annabelle Dixon, Mary Jane Drummond and Donald McIntyre (2004). *Learning without Limits* (Maidenhead: Open University Press).

Hattie, John (2009). *Visible Learning: A Synthesis of Over 800 Meta-Analyses Relating to Achievement* (Abingdon and New York: Routledge).

Hattie, John (2012). *Visible Learning for Teachers: Maximizing Impact on Learning* (Abingdon and New York: Routledge).

Hattie, John (2017). 'I could not care less about how you teach!' Speech given at researchEd conference, Melbourne, 1 July. Video available at: https://visible-learning.org/2017/08/john-hattie-how-you-teach-video/.

Hook, Pam (2016). *First Steps with SOLO Taxonomy: Applying the Model in Your Classroom* (Invercargill, NZ: Essential Resources).

Hymer, Barry and Mike Gershon (2014). *Growth Mindset Pocketbook* (Alresford: Teachers' Pocketbooks).

Kline, Nancy (1999). *Time to Think: Listening to Ignite the Human Mind* (London: Octopus Books).

Lyman, Frank (1981). The Responsive Classroom Discussion: The Inclusion of All Students. In Audrey Anderson (ed.), *Mainstreaming Digest* (College Park, MD: University of Maryland Press), pp. 109–113.

McNeil, Liz and Pam Hook (2012). *SOLO Taxonomy and Making Meaning Book 1: Text Purposes, Audiences and Ideas* (Invercargill, NZ: Essential Resources).

McNeil, Liz and Pam Hook (2012). *SOLO Taxonomy and Making Meaning Book 2: Language Features, Structure and Organisation* (Invercargill, NZ: Essential Resources).

McNeil, Liz and Pam Hook (2012). *SOLO Taxonomy and Making Meaning Book 3: Extended Texts and Thematic Studies* (Invercargill, NZ: Essential Resources).

Maguire, Eleanor A., Katherine Woollett and Hugo J. Spiers (2006). London Taxi Drivers and Bus Drivers: A Structural MRI and Neuropsychological Analysis, *Hippocampus*, 16(12): 1091–1101.

Marks, Rachel (2013). 'The Blue Table Means You Don't Have a Clue': The Persistence of Fixed-Ability Thinking and Practices in Primary Mathematics in English Schools, *Forum*, 55(1): 31–44. Available at: http://doi.org/10.2304/forum.2013.55.1.31.

Mikami, Amori Yee, Erik A. Ruzek, Christopher A. Hafen, Anne Gregory and Joseph P. Allen (2017). Perceptions of Relatedness with Classroom Peers Promote Adolescents' Behavioral Engagement and Achievement in Secondary School, *Journal of Youth and Adolescence*, 46(11): 2341–2354.

Morrison McGill, Ross (n.d.) #TeacherTalk, *Teacher Toolkit* [blog]. Available at: https://www.teachertoolkit.co.uk/teachertalk/.

National Research Council (2000). *How People Learn: Brain, Mind, Experience, and School: Expanded Edition* (Washington, DC: National Academies Press). Available at: https://doi.org/10.17226/9853.

Newkirk, Thomas (2012). *The Art of Slow Reading: Six Time-Honored Practices for Engagement* (Portsmouth, NH: Heinemann).

Nottingham, James (2017). *The Learning Challenge: How to Guide Your Students Through the Learning Pit to Achieve Deeper Understanding* (Thousand Oaks, CA: Corwin Publishing).

Rosenthal, Robert and Elisha Y. Babad (1985). Pygmalion in the Gymnasium, *Educational Leadership*, 43(1): 36–39.

Ryan, Richard M. and Cynthia L. Powelson (1991). Autonomy and Relatedness as Fundamental to Motivation and Education, *The Journal of Experimental Education*, 60(1): 49–66.

Ryan, Richard M. and Edward L. Deci (2000). Self-Determination Theory and the Facilitation of Intrinsic Motivation, Social Development, and Well-Being, *American Psychologist*, 55(1): 68–78.

Ryan, Richard M. and Edward L. Deci (2000). When Rewards Compete with Nature: The Undermining of Intrinsic Motivation and Self-Regulation. In Carol Sansone and Judith M.

Harackiewicz (eds), *Intrinsic and Extrinsic Motivation: The Search for Optimal Motivation and Performance* (San Diego, CA: Academic Press), pp. 13–54.

Santos, Edalmarys and Chad A. Noggle (2011). Synaptic Pruning. In Sam Goldstein and Jack A. Naglieri (eds), *Encyclopedia of Child Behavior and Development* (Boston, MA: Springer), pp. 1464–1465.

Savage, Jonathan (ed.) (2013). *The Guided Reader to Teaching and Learning Music* (Abingdon and New York: Routledge).

Schwartz, Katrina (2015). How to Weave Growth Mindset into School Culture, *Mind Shift* [blog] (2 October). Available at: https://www.kqed.org/mindshift/42159/how-to-weave-growth-mindset-into-school-culture.

Soul Pancake (2016). 'Kid President Presents the Scariest Thing in the World' [video] (27 October). Available at: https://www.youtube.com/watch?v=x9SwbLN-OvY&index=3&list=PLzvRx_johoA-YabI6FWcU-jL6nKA1Um-t.

Standards and Testing Agency (2018). *Early Years Foundation Stage Profile: 2019 Handbook*. Ref: STA/19/8311/e (10 December). Available at: https://www.gov.uk/government/publications/early-years-foundation-stage-profile-handbook.

Swann, Mandy, Alison Peacock, Susan Hart and Mary Jane Drummond (2012). *Creating Learning without Limits* (Maidenhead: Open University Press).

Tofade, Toyin, Jamie Elsner and Stuart T. Haines (2013). Best Practice Strategies for Effective Use of Questions as a Teaching Tool, *American Journal of Pharmaceutical Education*, 77(7), Article 155. Available at: https://www.ncbi.nlm.nih.gov/pmc/articles/PMC3776909/.

Tomlinson, Carol Ann and Tonya R. Moon (2013). *Assessment and Student Success in a Differentiated Classroom* (Alexandria, VA: ACSD).

Vygotsky, Lev (1978). Interaction Between Learning and Development. In Mary Gauvain and Michael Cole (eds), *Readings on the Development of Children* (New York: Scientific American Books), pp. 34–40. Available at: https://www.faculty.mun.ca/cmattatall/Vygotsky_1978.pdf.

Watson, Angela (2017). 7 Ways Teachers Can Push Past Imposter Syndrome, *The Cornerstone for Teachers* [blog] (12 November). Available at: https://thecornerstoneforteachers.com/truth-for-teachers-podcast/imposter-syndrome/.

Wiliam, Dylan and Paul Black (1990). *Inside the Black Box: Raising Standards Through Classroom Assessment* (London: GL Assessment Ltd.).

Wroe, Nicholas (2009). Laughing Matters, *The Guardian* (11 April). Available at: https://www.theguardian.com/culture/2009/apr/11/interview-john-lloyd-comedy-producer.

Yates, Shirley (2009). Teacher Identification of Student Learned Helplessness in Mathematics, *Mathematics Education Research Journal*, 21(3): 86–106.